Grammar and Usage Workbook

Grade 7

McDougal Littell
A HOUGHTON MIFFLIN COMPANY
Evanston, Illinois • Boston • Dallas

Special Features of the Grammar and Usage Workbook

- It contains a wealth of skill-building exercises in grammar, usage, capitalization, and punctuation.
- Each page focuses on one topic or skill. A brief instructional summary is followed by comprehensive reinforcement exercises.
- Key words and phrases are highlighted for greater clarity and ease of use.
- Each page corresponds to a part in the pupil text for easy reference.
- Grammar lessons are leveled. Form A introduces the skill. Form B extends the skill with more advanced exercises.
- Skills Assessment sheets may be used by the student for self-diagnosis and additional practice or by the teacher as a check for understanding.
- A proofreading practice activity is provided for each Grammar and Usage Handbook.

Printed in the United States of America.

ISBN 0-395-86392-9

2 3 4 5 6 7 8 9 10 – MDO – 02 01 00 99 98 97

Contents

Grammar and Usage Handbook

The Parts of a Sentence

A **sentence** is a group of words that expresses a complete thought. A sentence must have a subject and a predicate. The **subject** tells whom or what the sentence is about. The **predicate** tells something about the subject.

Subject *(who or what)*	**Predicate** *(what is said about the subject)*
The girls	watched television.
Some people	like cold weather.
Doug Henning	performs magic tricks.

Finding the Subjects and Predicates Draw a vertical line between the subject and the predicate of each of the following sentences.

Example Everyone|laughed.

1. The President held a news conference on the White House lawn.

2. Each contestant chose a number from the big glass jar.

3. The audience gave the brass band a standing ovation.

4. Joe enjoyed his first lesson on the electric guitar.

5 Pam listened very carefully to the strange news bulletin.

6. The student council voted three times on the motion.

7. Beth and Barry steamed an assortment of fresh vegetables.

8. An alligator slid quietly into the water.

9. Thunder rumbled in the distance.

10. Three dogs circled the water hole.

11. The predicate of a sentence tells something about the subject.

12. Susan quickly locked the garage door.

13. Each skier wore a silver jacket and a white cap.

14. Bob searched nervously in the dark for the switch.

15. The dishwasher chugged noisily in the kitchen.

16. Lizzie's teacher finally agreed with the results.

17. I built these model cars in my spare time.

18. Many walkers joined the hike into the high country.

19. The man with the clipboard asked some strange questions.

20. The team raised the money for new uniforms.

21. The dolphins delighted the crowds at the aquarium.

22. Fuzhou is a city in southeast China.

Simple Subjects and Predicates

The **subject** of a sentence tells *whom* or *what* the sentence is about. The **predicate** tells what the subject does or is.

In every sentence there are key words that form the basic framework of the sentence. The key word in the subject of a sentence is called the **simple subject**. It is the **subject** of the verb. The key word in the predicate is called the **simple predicate**. The simple predicate is the **verb**.

> The *girl* with the long hair *fell* down.
> (*Girl* tells who fell down. It is the simple subject. *Fell* tells what the subject did. It is the simple predicate, or verb.)

Finding the Verbs and Their Simple Subjects In each sentence, underline the simple subject once and the verb twice.

Example The dog barked loudly.

1. The train from Seattle pulled into the station at three o'clock.
2. Leslie knitted a blue and white sweater for her dad.
3. Colorful seashells littered the deserted beach.
4. Almost all beekeepers wear protective masks.
5. Rain fell steadily all day long.
6. Three jugglers in the main ring tossed hoops into the air.
7. That roan horse gallops with a limp.
8. Tom Sawyer found a secret hideout.
9. Stars twinkled brightly in the ebony sky.
10. The pilot landed the plane skillfully in the midst of the storm.
11. The horse in that field leaped easily over the fence.
12. The valuable kite hangs in the top of the tree.
13. Three beautiful, mysterious packages lay on the table.
14. Six climbers from Nevada reached the mountaintop.
15. Sarah's uncle explained his collection of seashells to us.
16. Dawn stared at the empty gas gauge.
17. Lionel's mother works at an investment firm.
18. The volcanic island of Krakatau exploded in 1883.
19. The Midway Islands consist of a coral atoll and two islets.
20. Jiang quarreled with my interpretation of the movie's ending.

Finding the Verb

A **verb** expresses an action, states that something exists, or links the subject with a description.

Sometimes verbs tell about action:

Warren *threw* the ball. We *walked* home.

Sometimes the action is one that you cannot see:

Melissa *wanted* a puppy. Tom *thought* about it.

Some verbs tell that something is or exists. Such verbs indicate a *state of being.* They link a subject to a description of the subject.

Karen *is* a violinist. How many coins *are* old?
Susan's dress *looked* new. Bill's song *sounds* nice.

Finding the Verbs Underline the verb in each of the following sentences. It may tell about an action you can see, an action you cannot see, or a state of being. Mark each action verb *A* and each state-of-being verb *S*.

Example Jennifer has (A) an older brother.

1. Our sun is an enormous ball of gas.

2. Planets, asteroids, meteoroids, and comets travel around it.

3. Earth is the third planet from the sun.

4. It is the fifth largest planet in the solar system.

5. Saturn's rings amazed the great astronomer Galileo.

6. At least eighteen moons circle Saturn.

7 One of these moons is larger the the planet Mercury.

8. A small, hot planet, Mercury is closest to the sun.

9. Jupiter, the largest planet, spins on its axis once every ten hours.

10. Thick clouds cover the planet Venus.

11. Some people call Venus the morning star or the evening star.

12. Venus looks brighter than any star in the sky, except the sun.

13. Scientists know little about the distant planets Uranus and Neptune.

14. Clyde Tombaugh discovered the remote planet Pluto in 1930.

15. "Shooting stars" are really meteors.

Main Verbs and Helping Verbs

A verb may consist of a **main verb** and one or more **helping verbs,** such as *am, is, are, was, were, be, been, has, have, had, do, does,* or *did.* A main verb and its helping verbs make up a **verb phrase.**

Tara had (HV) been (HV) watching (MV) the program.
(*Had* and *been* are helping verbs. *Watching* is the main verb. *Had been watching* is a verb phrase.)

To find the verb in a sentence,

1. Look for a word that tells the main action, expresses a state of being, or links the subject with a description.
2. Look for helping verbs such as *is, am, are, was, were, be, been, have, has, had, do, does, did, shall, will, should, would,* and *could.*
3. Look for all the parts that make up the verb phrase.

Identifying Main Verbs and Helping Verbs Underline the verbs in the following sentences. Mark the main verbs *MV* and the helping verbs *HV.*

Example Greta has (HV) forgotten (MV) her lunch.

1. Victor's parents have gotten him a new camera for his birthday.

2. Now, Victor can take a photography class.

3. He will go to the community center.

4. There, he can join a class.

5. A woman has been teaching the class.

6. Victor has heard about Marge's popular class.

7. She has been explaining light meters and time exposure.

8. Victor might become a wildlife photographer for *National Geographic* someday.

Identifying Subjects and Verb Phrases Underline the verb phrases in the following sentences. Draw two lines under the simple subject of each verb phrase.

Example Sarah's big brown dog has frightened the neighbors.

1. Because of the fog, the chartered plane had left an hour late.

2. The jack-o'-lantern was glimmering in the living-room window.

3. Kay has been chosen as leader of the debate team.

4. By December we will have been living here ten years.

Separated Parts of a Verb

Sometimes the parts of a verb are separated by words that are not verbs.

> The artist *has* already *finished* the painting.
> I *did* not *understand* your question.
> She *has*n't *arrived* yet.

Finding the Verb In each of the following sentences, the parts of the verb are separated by one or more words that are not part of the verb. Underline the parts of the verb.

Example We <u>had</u> not <u>seen</u> the game.

1. Nick had never rowed a boat before.
2. The mayor has surely heard the good news.
3. The electrician will probably fix the lights soon.
4. I haven't always liked Italian food.
5. Diane has recently photographed parts of the Florida Everglades.
6. Those horses had seldom, if ever, run more than a mile.
7. Just two days earlier, my grandmother had carefully repaired the vase.
8. Maria is probably leaving early.
9. That clay will quickly harden.
10. Eric doesn't usually beat me in tennis.

Using Verbs and Subjects On the lines provided, supply helping verbs **(HV)** and main verbs **(MV)** as directed.

1. The silver car ________________ easily ________________ the race.
   HV MV
2. Snow ________________ quickly ________________ the town.
   HV MV
3. For weeks she ________________ not ________________ any news.
   HV MV
4. Janet ________________ not ________________ the concert.
   HV MV
5. Bill ________________ often ________________ the bicycle.
   HV MV
6. I ________________ usually ________________ at four o'clock.
   HV MV
7. We ________________ never ________________ that program.
   HV MV
8. The skiers ________________ soon ________________ down the trail.
   HV MV

Compound Subjects and Compound Verbs

A **compound subject** or a **compound verb** has two or more parts.

Susan and *Jane* saw the movie.
Terry *sprang* from the board and *dove* into the pool.

Identifying Compound Subjects and Compound Verbs

Underline the subjects once and the verbs twice in the following sentences.

Example Marissa swims and dives equally well.

1. Gary and Jonathan practiced a piano duet.
2. Yoshi turned slowly and spoke in a quiet voice.
3. Terriers, poodles, and other small dogs make popular house pets.
4. The campers canoed, hiked, and swam almost every day.
5. Marilyn's aunt and uncle are fine speakers.
6. We framed and hung the pictures.
7. Cardboard, a ruler, and scissors will be needed for this project.
8. Juanita and Dan wrote an interesting report about the expedition.
9. Debbie, Mitchell, and Michelle are my cousins.
10. Gymnasts balance, tumble, and vault.
11. Lions, tigers, and bears are all wild animals.
12. Martha Graham choreographed and performed modern ballets.
13. The kettle gurgled and sputtered on the stove.
14. The sun appeared for a moment and then disappeared behind a cloud.
15. The ducks in the pond swam to the island and sat on the shore.
16. Cheryl and Mark went to Florida for their vacation.
17. The koala blinked sleepily and climbed higher up the tree.
18. All at once, our dog ran to the basement door and listened intently.
19. The store on the corner and the shop next door have closed.
20. The carpenters measured and cut the wood.
21. Roses and irises filled every vase in the house.
22. *The Simpsons* and *Nature* are Jeff's favorite programs.
23. With that, Nelson scowled and stormed out of the room.
24. In the summer our neighbors sit on the porch and drink lemonade.
25. The nurse took my temperature and checked my pulse.

Kinds of Sentences

There are four kinds of sentences: **declarative, interrogative, imperative,** and **exclamatory.**

1. A **declarative sentence** makes a statement. It tells something. A period is used after this kind of sentence.

   My brother caught several fish this morning.

2. An **interrogative sentence** asks a question. A question mark is used after this kind of sentence.

   Do you know how to clean them?

3. An **imperative sentence** tells or requests someone to do something. This kind of sentence usually ends with a period.

   Please help yourself to some fish.

4. An **exclamatory sentence** expresses strong feeling. An exclamation point is used at the end of this kind of sentence.

   They taste great!

Classifying Sentences Read the following sentences and decide what kind each one is. On the line provided, write the number of the correct sentence category. Then write the punctuation mark that belongs at the end.

Example __1__ Judy is my sister.

_____ **1.** The Sears Tower is the tallest building in the world

_____ **2.** Please give me the recipe for your clam chowder

_____ **3.** Did Thomas Jefferson write most of the Declaration of Independence

_____ **4.** The Incas made beautiful objects from precious metals

_____ **5.** What an amazing story she has told us

_____ **6.** Cancel my order

_____ **7.** Go tell it on the mountain

_____ **8.** Why do you suppose elephants have trunks

_____ **9.** Edgar Allan Poe is considered the father of the detective story

_____ **10.** How quickly this letter was delivered

Subjects in Unusual Order

The subject does not always come at the beginning of a sentence. Placing the verb before the subject can make your writing more interesting. It will also give more emphasis to what you say.

Usual Order	The jets sped into the deep blue sky.
Unusual Order	Into the deep blue sky sped the jets.

Finding the Subjects and Verbs In each of the following sentences, underline the subject once and the verb twice.

1. On and on, through the night, rode the messenger.
2. In the cockpit the pilot checked the instruments.
3. Over the bridge glided the sleigh.
4. In the garden the onions and tomatoes sprouted among the other vegetables.
5. Before us loomed a range of high mountains.
6. Above the horizon floated the parachute.
7. On a large lily pad a green frog caught insects.
8. Several photographs and candles were on the mantel.
9. Through the hollow log ran a chipmunk.
10. In the distance we could see a bright yellow car.
11. Beyond the trees, gleaming in the sun, flowed the wide river.
12. In the last row sat the author of the play.
13. From the kitchen drifted the delicious aroma of spaghetti sauce.
14. There in the street lay the missing wallet.
15. In the top branches of the tree sat a small monkey.
16. In the doorway stood a stranger.
17. Down the pole the firefighters slid.
18. Into the store burst the excited shoppers.
19. Through the window glowed the light from the fireplace.
20. In the junkyard lay a pile of old tires and rusty fenders.
21. Out of the fog loomed ghostly shapes.
22. Across the field galloped the young colts.
23. The porpoises and dolphins leaped through the hoop.
24. Beyond the rocks sailed a brilliant white schooner.
25. Onto the screen flashed yet another commercial.

Questions and Exclamations

Some interrogative sentences (questions) are written in the usual order, with the subject first and the verb second.

Subject	**Verb**	
Who	ordered	this sandwich?

However, in other questions the subject may fall between the helping verb and the main verb.

HV	**Subject**	**MV**	
Do	you	know	Ms. Fisher?

Some exclamatory sentences also change the order of the subject and verb.

V	**S**	
Was	I	worried!

Identifying Subjects and Verbs in Questions and Exclamations In each sentence below, underline the subject once and the verb twice. Remember to underline all parts of the verb.

1. Has the morning paper come yet?
2. Was the soup prepared according to the recipe?
3. By the end of the game, were we excited!
4. Has Renaldo cleaned all that junk out of his room?
5. Aren't you having breakfast this morning?
6. Have you seen those huge elephants in the circus?
7. After the long hike, was Amy thirsty!
8. Who will coach our team?
9. What a strange person he is!
10. Can you be here by four o'clock?
11. Did the bus get to school on time?
12. Do you understand the importance of algebra?
13. Man, was he confused!
14. Does that offer still stand?
15. Were you waiting for me outside the mall?
16. Is laughter his usual reaction to criticism?
17. Doesn't Esther like Mexican food?
18. Did Paco find my black and white sneakers?

Commands

An imperative sentence (command) usually begins with the verb. For example, in the command *Be careful,* the verb is the first word. The subject of the sentence is *you,* even though it is not expressed. We say that the subject *you* is understood.

Sometimes only one word is necessary to give a command. That word is the verb. The subject is still *you* (understood).

(You) Stop. *(You)* Look. *(You)* Listen.

Finding Subjects and Verbs in Questions, Exclamations, and Commands Underline the subjects once and the verbs twice in the following sentences. Be sure to underline all parts of the verb. If the subject is understood, write *(You)* after the sentence.

1. Answer the door, please.
2. Which bicycle looks the newest?
3. Don't get too close to the edge of the canyon.
4. What a month October has been!
5. Give me a break.
6. Have Audrey and Carmen told you about their latest adventure?
7. If possible, give me a call before your departure.
8. Sit down and help yourself to some peaches.
9. Did the officer question the suspects?
10. Hurry!
11. Have you seen those ancient ruins in the desert?
12. Beat the eggs carefully for a successful, light custard.
13. How beautiful the sky is this evening!
14. Put some spruce boughs and dry leaves under your sleeping bag.
15. Have you ever seen Saturn through a telescope?
16. Pay the bill and keep the change.
17. Boy, was I scared!
18. What a fool I am!
19. Look for the verb in this sentence.
20. Then find the subject.

Sentences with There

When **there** is used to begin a sentence or ask a question, it acts as an *introductory word. There* is not the subject.

> There was nobody home. (*Was* is the verb, and *nobody* is the subject.)
> Were there any fish in the lake? (*Were* is the verb, and *fish* is the subject.)
> In the middle of the night there was a storm. (Was is the verb, and storm is the subject.)

Identifying Subjects and Verbs Underline the subject once and the verb twice in each of the following sentences.

1. There are many fans of bluegrass music in this country.
2. Aren't there any books about Mike Fink in the library?
3. On top of the mountain there is a geodesic dome.
4. Will there be an eclipse of the sun next year?
5. There aren't any dandelion greens in my salad.
6. Could there be life on other worlds?
7. Are there many hermit crabs on this beach?
8. During the Civil War there was a battle between two ironclad ships.
9. Will there ever be a substitute for wool?
10. Isn't there a pot of gold at the end of the rainbow?

Completing a *There* Sentence Finish each sentence below. Add the correct punctuation.

1. Will there ever be ______________________________
2. There certainly was ______________________________
3. Has there been ______________________________
4. There is always ______________________________
5. Were there ______________________________
6. There often were ______________________________
7. Are there always ______________________________
8. Was there ever ______________________________

Sentence Fragments

A **sentence fragment** is a group of words that does not express a complete idea. A sentence fragment leaves out something important, such as the subject or the verb or both. You may wonder *What is this about?* or *What happened?*

Threw the ball. *(Who threw the ball?)*
Kevin and his brothers. *(What about them?)*
Around the corner. *(Who was? What happened?)*

Recognizing Sentences Write *Sentence* or *Fragment* after each of the following.

1. At the first performance of the new band ______________

2. Expertly, Donna dribbled the ball ______________

3. Wondered about the gyroscope ______________

4. The hockey stick standing in the corner of the closet ______________

5. Roberto sang ______________

6. During the time of volcanic eruptions ______________

7. Bring your old shoes ______________

8. On the first voyage to Mars ______________

9. A plane landed ______________

10. A jumping mouse ______________

Completing Fragments Correct each of the following fragments by adding the words needed to make a sentence.

1. ______________________________ followed along on his bike.

2. After the storm ______________________________.

3. The cat and the dog ______________________________.

4. Near our house ______________________________.

5. ______________________________ after school today.

6. Next weekend, ______________________________.

Run-on Sentences

A **run-on sentence** occurs when two or more sentences are written as one. Sometimes no end mark is placed at the end of the first thought. At other times, a comma is incorrectly used.

Incorrect	The train was late we waited an hour.
Incorrect	The train was late, we waited an hour.
Correct	The train was late. We waited an hour.

Correcting Run-on Sentences If a group of words is a complete sentence, write *Sentence.* If it is a run-on, rewrite it correctly.

1. Lava shoots out of an erupting volcano.

____

2. People fear volcanoes, some eruptions have killed many.

____

3. The lava is very hot, its temperature may be above 2,000 degrees Fahrenheit. ______________________________

____

4. Large rocks burst out of volcanoes, these are called bombs.

____

5. The world's largest volcano is Mauna Loa in Hawaii.

____

6. In A.D. 79, Mount Vesuvius erupted, three towns were destroyed.

____

7. Scientists who study volcanoes are called volcanologists.

____

8. Volcanologists predict eruptions with a tiltmeter.

____

9. Mount St. Helens erupted in 1980, more than sixty people died.

____

10. Aconcagua in South America is an inactive volcano.

____

Linking Grammar and Writing: Understanding Sentences

Imagine that you have spent many hours observing the activity of an ant colony for a science project. Some of the notes you have taken are listed below. Turn these notes into a well-written paragraph. First write a rough draft on another sheet of paper, making sure that every sentence in your paragraph is complete. Include at least one exclamatory sentence, one interrogative sentence, and two sentences with subjects and verbs in unusual order. In your final draft, draw one line under the subject and two lines under the verb of each sentence.

large anthill along crack in sidewalk
about twenty ants working around hill
black segmented bodies, waving feelers
swarm around large bread crumb near hill
drag smaller crumbs into hill (terrible struggle!)
favorite food: sugar
sprinkled thin line of sugar near hill
ants abandoned bread crumbs

Additional Practice: Understanding Sentences

Correcting Run-ons and Fragments The following paragraphs contain sentence fragments and run-on sentences. Rewrite the paragraphs, fixing the fragments and run-ons.

Videotape. Has many advantages over film. First of all, a videotape does not have to be developed it can be played back immediately on a VCR. Second, videotape records. Both picture and sound. Finally, the tape can be erased it can be used over again.

Videotape systems have become popular. People record television shows. To watch at a more convenient time. Rental tapes of popular movies are also widely available. Videotape cameras are used like movie cameras, people are using them to record family events. A videotape system is a useful addition to any television set.

Review: Understanding Sentences

Identifying Subjects and Verbs Underline the subjects once and the verbs twice in the following sentences. Insert the proper punctuation at the end of each sentence. If the subject is understood to be *you,* write *(You)* after the sentence.

1. The frisky colt trotted into the yard and laid its head on my shoulder
2. Have you ever heard of the ancient city of Byzantium
3. Stop that at once
4. Isn't the Big Dipper part of the constellation Ursa Major
5. Ask me no questions
6. Should there always be nuts and raisins in a good fruitcake
7. Argentine gauchos and North American cowboys were expert riders of horses
8. George Gershwin wrote several musicals and composed an opera
9. Is there a doctor in the house
10. The modern nation of Israel came into existence in 1948
11. Boomerangs have been used for hunting since ancient times
12. Didn't the trumpeter swan almost become extinct
13. After Hanukah and Christmas comes New Year's Day
14. Can there ever be an end to war
15. Volleyball has been an Olympic sport since 1964
16. Act soon

Recognizing Sentences, Fragments, and Run-ons Each of the following groups of words is a *sentence, a fragment,* or a *run-on.* Identify each by writing *S, F,* or *R* on the line provided.

_____ 1. Worked out last night at the gym.

_____ 2. The noise bothered us we couldn't think.

_____ 3. Are there any other volunteers?

_____ 4. Helped us with our work.

_____ 5. Come over after school.

_____ 6. Dictionaries give definitions, they are helpful to writers.

_____ 7. Use the soap and the towels in the left drawer.

_____ 8. The firefighters on the way to the fire.

What Is a Noun?

A **noun** names a person, a place, a thing, or an idea.

Things named by nouns may be things you can see:

chair   tree   Crystal Lake   Mexico   light

Other things named by nouns may be emotions you can feel:

anger   sadness   happiness   love   confusion

Still other things named by nouns are ideas:

friendship   fairness   honesty   freedom   truth

Identifying Nouns Underline the nouns in each of the following sentences. Each sentence has more than one noun.

1. Snow covers the top of Mount Rainier.
2. The chair my grandfather carved was a labor of love.
3. Grasshoppers have strong muscles in their legs.
4. The hurdy-gurdy is a musical instrument with strings and a wheel.
5. Absence makes the heart grow fonder.
6. Slender saplings danced in the wind.
7. Orangutans live in trees and rarely come down to the ground.
8. Hurricanes in some places are called typhoons or tropical cyclones.
9. Has your sister read any of Mark Twain's books?
10. Charity begins at home.
11. Spring comes earlier to St. Louis than to Chicago.
12. Suddenly an owl screeched in the darkness.
13. The Pacific Ocean reaches a depth of nearly seven miles.
14. Zimbabwe, Senegal, and Nigeria are independent African states.
15. Beauty is in the eye of the beholder, according to an old saying.
16. Wallace Stevens wrote "The Man with the Blue Guitar."
17. Julie has a fondness for chocolate.
18. "Some say the world will end in fire, / Some say in ice."
19. Carlos can make beautiful fabrics with his loom.
20. A few snakes have traces of hind limbs.
21. The game of soccer goes back many centuries in England.
22. Termites, or white ants, can do great damage to a wooden building.

Common Nouns and Proper Nouns

A **common noun** names a whole class of persons, places, things, or ideas. It is a general name and does not refer to a special person, place, thing, or idea. A **proper noun** names a particular person, place, thing, or idea. A proper noun always begins with a capital letter. It may also consist of more than one word.

Common Nouns	Proper Nouns
girl	Julie Anderson
road	Buffalo Grove Road
store	Flora's Garden Shop

Finding the Proper Nouns Capitalize the proper nouns in the following sentences.

Example julio went to chicago. (J, C)

1. They live near the choctawhatchee river in florida.
2. The ferry to staten island passes near a famous statue.
3. One postcard was from sequoia national park.
4. The writer flannery o'connor was born in georgia.
5. In williamsburg, we can see how americans once lived.
6. Toronto and montreal are major cities in Canada.
7. A famous address in london is 10 downing street.
8. The jefferson library is equipped with computers now.
9. The cajuns of louisiana were originally from nova scotia.
10. The coast of new england has many fishing ports.

Determining Proper Nouns For each common noun that is given, write an appropriate proper noun on the line.

1. month ____________________
2. neighbor ____________________
3. actor ____________________
4. city ____________________
5. movie ____________________
6. country ____________________
7. cereal ____________________
8. holiday ____________________
9. scientist ____________________
10. vehicle ____________________

Nouns Used as Subjects

A **noun** may be used as the *subject* of a sentence. The subject of a sentence tells who or what is being talked about.

> Anita entered the room quietly.
>
> Thousands filled the stadium.

Sometimes the subject is not placed next to the verb. Other words may separate them. Occasionally the subject is at the end of the sentence.

> Anita always entered the room quietly.
>
> Thousands of Lakers fans filled the stadium.
>
> Beyond the mountains lay only desert.

Finding Nouns Used as Subjects Underline each of the nouns used as subjects.

1. My sister is my favorite singer.
2. From behind the heavy red curtain stepped the radiant ballerina.
3. The pen with the felt tip wrote well.
4. Cinnamon is made from the bark of trees native to the East Indies and Southeast Asia.
5. Into the clear blue pond waddled a large, quacking duck.
6. The members of the debating team were satisfied with their performance.
7. There were several players chosen for Saturday's racquetball tournament.
8. Detective Richards followed the clues on the faded old map.
9. That woman just became the new school-district superintendent.
10. The scrimmage lasted one hour.
11. There was only one solution to the puzzle.
12. My cousin entered this year's Special Olympics.
13. Out of the acacia tree flew a colorful bird.
14. The bicycle in the garage has a flat tire.
15. In southwestern Switzerland, on the French border, is Lake Geneva.
16. Jackals are wild dogs that hunt in packs.
17. According to Greek legend, Priam was the last king of Troy.
18. Lindsay did fifty sit-ups in class this morning.

Nouns Used as Direct Objects

A noun used as a *direct object* receives the action of a verb.

Gary threw the *ball.* (What did Gary throw? The *ball.*)
Angie saw the *dentist.* (Whom did Angie see? The *dentist.*)
We have a *surprise* for you. (What do we have? A *surprise.*)

Identifying Direct Objects Underline the noun used as a direct object in each of the following sentences.

1. The satellite is circling the earth.
2. Ms. Steinberg needed a new compass.
3. The sparrow chased a gigantic crow from the apple tree.
4. We saw a picture of Harriet Tubman in the library.
5. St. George slew the ferocious dragon.
6. Did you understand the assignment?
7. Follow the leader of that cleanup team.
8. Some elephants have enormous tusks.
9. That man in the chef's cap prepared a smorgasbord for our party.
10. That sentence has a curious mistake in it.
11. The octopus grasped a rock with one of its tentacles.
12. My cousins and I ate lunch on the wharf.
13. Speedy Messenger Service delivered a long telegram to the senator.
14. Ms. Phelps parked her car in front of the hardware store.
15. Who bought this Scott Joplin album?
16. The child nearly lost her way in the dark.
17. Kings ruled the early Sumerian cities.
18. Mr. Thies argued the case in court.
19. Each word has three syllables.
20. Who leads the National League in home runs?
21. Clara and Mark sang a duet on the front lawn.
22. Mix a batch of granola for tomorrow's breakfast.
23. During intermission, a mime provided humorous relief.
24. The raccoon has a long black-ringed tail.
25. Alex quizzed Judith about her knowledge of reptiles.

Nouns Used as Indirect Objects

The **indirect object** of a verb generally tells to whom or for whom an action is done.

Jennifer gave *Robert* the book. (*Robert* is the indirect object.)

A sentence may contain an indirect object only if it also contains a direct object. The indirect object comes before the direct object and says to whom (or to what) or for whom (or for what) something is done. The word *to* or *for* never appears before an indirect object.

Finding Indirect Objects Underline the nouns used as indirect objects in the following sentences.

1. Zev showed Paula the latest dance step.
2. The school mailed the new students their registration forms.
3. Some horses give trainers many problems.
4. We should have told Eric and Joan the truth.
5. Sylvia gave her car an oil change.
6. The pitcher threw the batter a curve.
7. In the afternoon the lion brought its mate some food.
8. The governor promised the town some financial aid in the coming year.
9. Every year Juan gives the children presents.
10. The teacher read the class a short story.
11. My mother bought our family a new chess set.
12. Dr. Shirish showed her assistant the new procedure.
13. Michael sent the president and the governor a letter about the proposed dam.
14. The wrestling coach told the team the rules.
15. Write Karen a letter about your plans for the future.
16. The principal found my brother and sister jobs for the summer.
17. Will you show the artist your painting?
18. Last summer Dad gave Jane a calculator for her birthday.
19. I'll knit Mom a sweater for her next birthday.
20. Ms. Perkins showed the students the costumes for the play.
21. The host served the guests chilled cucumber soup.
22. Give that nail a good whack.
23. The accident taught the sailors an important lesson.
24. Will you show the electrician the location of the fuse box?

Predicate Nouns

A **predicate noun** is a noun in the predicate that explains or identifies the subject. When a linking verb connects the subject of a sentence with a noun in the predicate, that word is a predicate noun. It usually refers to the same thing as the subject. In many cases, if the predicate noun and the subject are exchanged, the resulting sentence will still make sense.

The dog is a *dachshund.* (*Dachshund* is a predicate noun.)

The *dachshund* is a dog. (Now *dachshund* is the subject.)

Finding Predicate Nouns On the line provided, write *PN,* for *Predicate Noun,* or *DO,* for *Direct Object,* to describe the word in italics.

Example Anthony was a detective. PN
Anthony hired a detective. DO

_____ **1.** That morning Nikki entered the *classroom* five minutes late.

_____ **2.** The whole outdoors became our *classroom* for a day.

_____ **3.** Ronnie has been my best *friend* ever since our childhood.

_____ **4.** I have found that she will always help a *friend.*

_____ **5.** Sirius, the Dog Star, is the brightest *star* in the sky.

_____ **6.** Jerry visited a Hollywood set and met the *star* of the movie.

_____ **7.** The coach looked us over carefully before she chose the *team.*

_____ **8.** Laurel and Hardy were a very funny *team* in early films.

Identifying Predicate Nouns Underline the predicate nouns in the following sentences. If a sentence does not have a predicate noun, write *None* after the sentence.

1. The ancestors of the Inuit people were Asians.

2. They had probably crossed the Bering Sea in umiaks.

3. Umiaks are large boats made of skin.

4. Long ago, the Inuits became skilled and efficient hunters.

5. They are also talented storytellers.

6. Most of their stories have been traditional tales.

7. The tales describe Inuit life in a harsh climate.

8. They also tell about courage and love of family.

9. Inuit stories are a record of the past for young people.

10. Many of the tales are passed down from one generation to the next.

The Plurals of Nouns

A **singular noun** names one person, place, thing, or idea. A **plural noun** names more than one person, place, thing, or idea.

Here are seven rules for forming the plurals of nouns:

1. To form the plural of most nouns, add *-s.*

streets houses cousins bowls

2. When the singular ends in *s, sh, ch, x,* or *z,* add *-es.*

hisses brushes torches boxes buzzes

3. When the singular ends in *o,* add *-s.*

radios stereos sopranos silos

Exceptions: For a few words ending in *o* preceded by a consonant, add *-es:* tomatoes, heroes, potatoes, echoes.

4. When a singular noun ends in *y* preceded by a consonant, change the *y* to *i* and add *-es.*

hobby—hobbies cry—cries party—parties

If the *y* is preceded by a vowel, do not change the *y* to *i.* Just add *-s* to the singular.

boy—boys monkey—monkeys day—days valley—valleys

5. For most nouns ending in *f,* add *-s.* For some nouns ending in *f* or *fe,* however, change the *f* to *v* and add *-es* or *-s.*

roof—roofs cuff—cuffs shelf—shelves knife—knives

6. Some nouns are spelled the same in the singular and the plural.

moose deer sheep tuna

7. The plurals of some nouns are formed in ways that are unusual or unique.

man—men foot—feet mouse—mice woman—women

Forming Plurals Write the plural of each of the following nouns. Use a dictionary to check your work.

1. bridge ____________________ **6.** cello ____________________

2. staff ____________________ **7.** moose ____________________

3. alley ____________________ **8.** bench ____________________

4. church ____________________ **9.** century ____________________

5. family ____________________ **10.** life ____________________

Possessive Nouns

A **possessive noun** shows who or what owns something. It shows that something belongs to or is a part of someone or something.

Judy's talent   my *father's* hat

To form the possessive of a singular noun, add an apostrophe and *-s.*

Judy—Judy's   father—father's   waitress—waitress's

To form the possessive of a plural noun that ends in *s,* just add an apostrophe.

ladies—ladies'   runners—runners'

To form the possessive of a plural noun that does not end in *s,* add an apostrophe and *-s.*

children—children's   women—women's

Writing Possessive Forms of Nouns On each line write a more concise form of the phrase, using a possessive noun.

1. legs of a grasshopper ______________________

2. father of Cindy ______________________

3. alphabet of the Greeks ______________________

4. association of men ______________________

5. pencils of a student ______________________

6. secretary of a senator ______________________

7. end of a year ______________________

8. shoes of ladies ______________________

9. stings of bees ______________________

10. interests of women ______________________

11. complaints of students ______________________

12. shoes of a man ______________________

13. membership of churches ______________________

14. wing of a fly ______________________

15. friend of Charles ______________________

Linking Grammar and Writing: Using Nouns

One Saturday you are helping out at Frank's Place, a diner belonging to your uncle. Four of your friends come in and place a *very* confusing order. Each person orders a hamburger or hot dog fixed a different way, along with at least three other items.

Item	Price	Item	Price
Frankfurter	$1.25	Baked Potato	$1.00
Chili Frank	1.60	Onions	.15
Frankenburger	1.75	Chili	.45
Double Frankenburger	2.80		
		Frankly Fantastic Yogurt	1.25
Extras			
Cheese	.25		
Hot Peppers	.25		
Sweet Peppers	.25	Beverages	.65, .85

On the lines below, write the names of four friends and a description of each order as the person might have given it. Use complete sentences to describe each order. Underline each noun.

1. ______________________ : ______________________________________

____

____

2. ______________________ : ______________________________________

____

____

3. ______________________ : ______________________________________

____

____

4. ______________________ : ______________________________________

____

____

Additional Practice: Using Nouns

Identifying Nouns and Their Uses On the lines, write the nouns in the sentences. Next to each noun, describe how it is used by writing *S* (subject), *DO* (direct object), *IO* (indirect object), or *PN* (predicate noun).

1. Captain Davenport is our most experienced pilot.

____

2. Keith told Harriet a long, boring joke.

____

3. The gardener pruned and watered the young trees.

____

4. Lucy and Audrey taught their parents chess.

____

5. The officer gave both drivers tickets and friendly advice.

____

Using Plurals and Possessives Correctly The following sentences contain ten errors in plural and possessive forms of nouns. Find the errors and rewrite each sentence correctly.

1. A herd of deers approached my families' campsite.

____

2. Dishes from country's around the world are served at Alices restaurant.

____

3. Important Aztec chieves wore cloak's of legendary beauty.

____

4. Mr. Lopez's store has a sale on FM radioes.

____

5. Sabrina changed Herbies' recipe by substituting tomatos and bay leafs.

____

Review: Using Nouns

Finding Nouns Underline the nouns in the sentences below. Above each noun, write *S* (subject), *DO* (direct object), or *IO* (indirect object) to describe how the noun is used.

Example Ted (S) gave Elaine (IO) the wrong book (DO).

1. Governor Reeves and the committee sent our school a special award.

2. Did Buddy give his brother and sister advice?

3. The assistant handed the carpenter a hammer.

4. Juanita gave the neighbors some vegetables and fruit.

Identifying Predicate Nouns Underline the predicate noun in each sentence.

1. Millie is the captain of our volleyball team this year.

2. Such a hasty decision might be a mistake.

3. The three-mile run was a difficult challenge for us.

4. Our house is the oldest building on the block.

Forming Plurals and Possessives On the line provided, write the plural or the possessive form, as directed, for each of the nouns.

1. deer (plural) ____________________

2. shelf (plural) ____________________

3. Chris (singular possessive) ____________________

4. driver (plural possessive) ____________________

5. child (plural possessive) ____________________

6. hero (plural possessive) ____________________

7. wife (plural) ____________________

8. tooth (plural) ____________________

9. actress (singular possessive) ____________________

10. lady (plural possessive) ____________________

What Is a Pronoun?

A **pronoun** is a word used to take the place of a noun or another pronoun. Pronouns have three forms: *subject, object,* and *possessive.*

The *boys* cut the tree.	*They* cut the tree.	(subject)
Willie thanked *Fay.*	Willie thanked *her.*	(direct object)
Where is *Ed's* book?	Where is *his* book?	(possessive)

The pronouns listed below are called **personal pronouns.** Each has a subject, an object, and a possessive form—for example, *I, me,* and *my.*

	Subject	**Object**	**Possessive**
Singular	I, you, she, he, it	me, you, her, him, it	my, mine, your, yours, her, hers, his, its
Plural	we, you, they	us, you, them	our, ours, your, yours, their, theirs

Using Pronouns Correctly Rewrite the following sentences, changing the proper nouns to pronouns and following the other directions.

Example Mary gave Chris and Harry some paper. (You are Mary; use one word for *Chris and Harry.*)

I gave them some paper.

1. The bike belongs to Carlos. (You are not Carlos; use a pronoun for *The bike.*)

____

2. The Fishers gave Karyn a party. (You are not Karyn; use one word for *The Fishers.*)

____

3. Show Vicki the program. (You are Vicki.)

____

4. George will give Angela the book that belongs to Angela. (You are George, and you are talking to Angela.)

____

5. Toby's father gave Toby's bike to Jill and Amy. (You are Toby; use one word for *Jill and Amy.*)

____

6. Keith put Sherry's backpack in the hall closet. (You are Keith, and you are talking to Sherry.)

____

Subject Pronouns

The pronouns *I, you, he, she, it, we,* and *they* are **subject pronouns.** Use them as subjects of sentences or after linking verbs.

The subject form of a pronoun is used as the subject of a sentence or as a predicate pronoun following a linking verb. A **predicate pronoun** is a pronoun that renames, or refers to, the subject.

Subjects	**Predicate Pronouns**
You and *I* won.	The winners were *you* and *I.*

Here are some points to remember about predicate pronouns:

1. Predicate pronouns follow linking verbs such as *am, is, are, was, were, shall be,* and *will be.*
2. A predicate pronoun renames, or refers to, the subject of the sentence.
3. A sentence with a predicate pronoun will usually make sense if the subject and the predicate pronoun are reversed.

   The kicker was *he.*
   He was the kicker.

Always use subject forms of pronouns for subjects and predicate pronouns.

Incorrect The runner was *her.*
Correct The runner was *she.*

Choosing the Right Pronoun Underline the correct forms of the subject and predicate pronouns.

1. Billy and (she, her) went to the basketball game.

2. The most excited spectators were (we, us).

3. Mary Leakey and (they, them) searched for fossils in Tanzania.

4. The real victims of the plot were (she, her) and her family.

5. The skaters who had practiced the hardest were José and (we, us).

6. Two of the biggest Giants fans were (he, him) and (I, me).

7. The dog trainer we admired the most was (she, her).

8. Mary and (he, him) were first-rate wildlife photographers.

9. The leaders of the backpacking trip will be (he, him) and (she, her).

10. The best hockey player on the team was (she, her).

11. In Arizona, (she, her) and Carmen rode a dune buggy.

12. The man slicing green beans for dinner is (he, him).

13. Mike and (I, me) stared at the hedgehog.

14. The proprietors of the feed store are (she, her) and her father.

Object Pronouns

The pronouns *me, you, him, her, it, us,* and *them* are **object pronouns.** Use them as objects of verbs or as objects of prepositions.

Direct Object	Larry helped *her.*
Indirect Object	Sally asked *me* a question.
Object of Preposition	Carlos gave the keys to *them.*

A compound object may consist of two pronouns, or a noun and a pronoun, connected by *and, or,* or *nor.* The object forms of pronouns are used in all compound objects.

Direct Object	Ted thanked *Terry* and *me.*
Indirect Object	Give *Alice* and *me* a hand.
Object of Preposition	I made the sweaters for *you* and *her.*

Choosing the Correct Pronoun as Object Underline the correct pronouns in the following sentences. Label each pronoun *DO* (direct object), *IO* (indirect object), or *OP* (object of preposition).

1. The soldier at the gate saluted Jimmy and (he, him).
2. When will you send (she, her) and (I, me) the yellow yarn?
3. All the skiers followed (they, them) and (we, us) down the slope.
4. The shifting wind at the summit hit (she, her) from all sides.
5. Phoebe showed the Indian arrowhead to Patty and (we, us).
6. The archaeologist helped (they, them) at the dig.
7. Rick met Lois and (she, her) at the international airport.
8. Please give the boarding passes to (they, them).
9. The veterinarian told Anita and (we, us) about chimpanzees.
10. The host of the party greeted (he, him) and (I, me) at the door.
11. We had all heard good things about (he, him) and his brother.
12. Dad gave Toshi and (he, him) a ride to the soccer game.
13. The master of ceremonies awarded Bev and (I, me) the second prize.
14. Some in the audience had questions for (we, us) and the rest of the cast.
15. The mysterious stranger asked (he, him) and (she, her) for directions.
16. Luckily, Jason had taught (they, them) the Heimlich maneuver.
17. Denise mailed the package to (we, us) at the old address.
18. Did you show Brian and (he, him) your new tool set?
19. Uncle Irving told (I, me) a funny story about (she, her).
20. Janet made an ice sculpture for the twins and (we, us).

Possessive Pronouns and Contractions

Possessive pronouns are personal pronouns used to show ownership or belonging. Unlike possessive nouns, the possessive forms of pronouns have no apostrophes.

my, mine	our, ours
your, yours	your, yours
his, her, hers, its	their, theirs

Many people confuse the possessive forms of some pronouns with the contractions they resemble. Pairs often confused include *its* and *it's, your* and *you're,* and *their* and *they're.* Remember that possessive pronouns do not have apostrophes.

The dog lost *its* tags.	The twins rode *their* bikes.
It's raining again.	*They're* riding bikes.

Using Possessive Forms Correctly Underline the correct forms in the following sentences.

1. For several days the oriole prepared a nest for (it's, its) young.

2. The Smiths are probably home, since that car is (their's, theirs).

3. (You're, Your) going to enter that poster contest, aren't you?

4. Since (it's, its) rained for over a week, our street is flooded.

5. Is (they're, their) latest album out yet?

6. Is (you're, your) robot able to move (it's, its) arm?

7. Let's walk to school if (it's, its) warm today.

8. (They're, Their) newspaper was wet, so (it's, its) pages stuck together.

9. The lambs stood unsteadily beside (they're, their) mother.

10. (They're, Their) French Canadians, living in the city of Quebec.

11. Does (you're, your) Siamese cat have blue eyes?

12. Our maple tree lost (it's, its) leaves early this fall.

13. Please tell me when (it's, its) time to light the oven.

14. Tony put the unabridged dictionary back on (it's, its) shelf.

15. If (you're, your) going to the picnic, sign up here.

16. My lasagna recipe calls for mushrooms; does (your's, yours)?

17. (They're, Their) outside, trying out (they're, their) new bikes.

18. Okapis are related to giraffes, but (they're, their) necks are shorter.

19. His saddle shoes are newer than (her's, hers).

20. (It's, Its) time to give the goldfish (it's, its) food.

Pronoun Problems

When do you say *we boys* and *we girls?* When do you say *us boys* and *us girls?* You will make the correct choice if you try the pronoun alone in the sentence.

(We, Us) girls hiked along the beach.
(*We* hiked. Therefore, "*We girls* hiked" is correct.)

We is always the subject form; **us** is the object form.

Who and *whom*, when used to ask questions, are called **interrogative pronouns. Who** is the subject form; **whom** is the object form.

Who will perform the song?	(*Who* is the subject of the verb *perform.*)
Whom did the captain choose?	(*Whom* is the direct object of *did choose.*)
For *whom* did you vote?	(*Whom* is the object of the preposition *for.*)

Using the Correct Pronoun Underline the correct pronoun in each of the following sentences.

1. The weather report is giving (we, us) skiers some hope for more snow.
2. (Who, Whom) was the first to find a pass through these mountains?
3. Ted's mother gave (we, us) boys a cooking lesson today.
4. (We, Us) campers cleared a trail to Crystal Lake.
5. Did you see (we, us) students at the botanical garden?
6. (Who, Whom) did you ask to feed the cats while we are away?
7. (We, Us) runners like the outdoor track better.
8. (Who, Whom) started all the trouble in the Balkan states?
9. That dog just followed (we, us) boys home.
10. Do you know (who, whom) the secretary of state is?
11. Librarians can help (we, us) students find what we're looking for.
12. (Who, Whom) did the British elect as prime minister?
13. In a flash (we, us) divers saw the danger, but it was too late.
14. We hope that they will not forget (we, us) left-handers.
15. (We, Us) dancers will perform the opening number tonight.
16. (Who, Whom) did Grant Wood paint in *American Gothic?*
17. (We, Us) swimmers were able to get help for the injured sea gull.
18. For (who, whom) did you say you bought those earrings?
19. (Who, Whom) painted that big mural in the post office?
20. Could you show (we, us) visitors where the King Tut exhibit is?

Reflexive and Intensive Pronouns

Pronouns that end in ***-self*** or ***-selves*** are either intensive or reflexive pronouns. They are *myself, yourself, herself, himself, itself, ourselves, yourselves,* and *themselves.*

A **reflexive pronoun** refers to an action of the subject of a sentence. The meaning of the sentence is incomplete without the pronoun.

> Ask *yourself* if you really need to go. (Without *yourself,* the meaning of the sentence is incomplete.)

An **intensive pronoun** adds emphasis to a noun or another pronoun. The meaning of a sentence is complete without it.

> Carmen *herself* spoke before the group. (Even without *herself,* the meaning of the sentence remains complete.)

Using Reflexive and Intensive Pronouns Complete each sentence by writing the correct reflexive or intensive pronoun on the line provided. After each sentence write *R* (reflexive) or *I* (intensive).

1. Let's give ________________ a fighting chance to win this game.

2. If left alone, this problem may just solve ________________ .

3. I ________________ will testify if it will help your case.

4. The students ________________ must make their views known now.

5. Be careful that you don't cut ________________ on that sharp blade.

6. The wheel bearing ________________ may need to be replaced.

7. Atsuko introduced ________________ to as many voters as he could.

8. Around here, the only person who plays chess well is Maria ________________ .

9. It is we ________________ who must speak out about the cheating.

10. We hope she will not blame ________________ for the misunderstanding.

11. If you and your friends find any ripe peaches, help ________________ .

12. I know ________________ well enough to stay away from the candy store.

13. Mr. Bacon ________________ told us that the pool was closed.

14. You ________________ could be your own worst enemy.

Pronouns and Their Antecedents

The **antecedent** of a pronoun is the noun or other pronoun for which that pronoun stands. The antecedent usually appears before the pronoun, sometimes even in the sentence before it.

The *architect* came today and brought *her* drawings.
(*Architect* is the antecedent of *her.*)
Debby and *Tom* came in. *They* were laughing.
(*Debby* and *Tom* are the antecedents of *they.*)

Pronouns must agree with their antecedents. Use a singular pronoun for a singular antecedent. Use a plural pronoun for a plural antecedent.

The *Book of Kells* (singular) is a beautiful old gospel manuscript.
It (singular) is in Dublin, Ireland.
Some *snakes* (plural) make *their* (plural) homes in trees.

Finding the Antecedents Underline the pronouns in the following sentences. Circle each pronoun's antecedent and draw an arrow to it.

Example (Janice) rode her bicycle.

1. Uncle Jack is driving a new pickup truck. He just bought it.
2. The Erie Canal is used for barges. It allows them to be moved quickly.
3. Marc should carry his own backpack.
4. Mandy brought her skateboard with her.
5. Istanbul is a great city in Turkey. Its former name was Constantinople.
6. Did Chung find his jacket? It's in his room.

Using Pronouns with Antecedents Complete the following sentences with the correct pronouns.

1. Anita put a van Gogh print on __________ wall because __________ liked __________ bright colors.
2. Mr. Lee moved __________ lawn sprinkler because __________ was getting water on __________ car. __________ dragged __________ over near the bushes.
3. Elliot had rice, beans, and spices in __________ kitchen. __________ mixed __________ to make a New Orleans–style dish.
4. Kim and Tina put __________ return bottles on the counter. __________ got a dollar and gave all of __________ to __________ little brother.

Indefinite Pronouns

An **indefinite pronoun** is a pronoun that does not refer to a particular person or thing. Some indefinite pronouns are singular. Others are plural.

Singular Indefinite Pronouns			Plural Indefinite Pronouns	
another	each	everything	one	both
anybody	either	neither	somebody	few
anyone	everybody	nobody	someone	many
anything	everyone	no one	something	several

Use the singular possessive pronouns *his, her,* and *its* with singular indefinite pronouns. Use the plural possessive pronoun *their* with plural indefinite pronouns.

Using Indefinite Pronouns Correctly Underline the correct possessive pronoun in each sentence. Circle its antecedent.

Example Someone left (his or her, their) pen here.

1. Before the math test, anyone can look at (his or her, their) book.
2. Neither of the girls was at (her, their) best in the swim meet.
3. Both of the boys inherited (his, their) mother's red hair.
4. Sooner or later, everyone must make (his or her, their) own decisions.
5. Each of the rabbits has (its, their) own pen.
6. At the trial, each of the witnesses told (his or her, their) story.
7. Many brought (their, her) own lunches.
8. Someone canceled (his, their) subscription to that skateboarding magazine.
9. Is there anybody who will donate (her, their) time to the neighborhood cleanup?
10. After lunch, everybody went (her, their) own way.
11. Few in our class have reached (his or her, their) full height.
12. Neither of the contestants chose (her, their) best category.
13. Several of the trees were losing (its, their) leaves.
14. No one had (her, their) proper supplies for the cookout.
15. Each of the cars had (its, their) headlights dimmed in the thick fog.
16. Few of the students have completed (his or her, their) term papers yet.
17. Somebody left (their, his or her) address book on the window ledge.
18. Either Ahmad or Roger will lead (their, his) team to victory.

Linking Grammar and Writing: Using Pronouns

The people who create a television commercial begin by planning the entire commercial. They describe each scene in detail, telling what images will appear on the screen and what the characters will say.

Imagine that you have been hired to think up a commercial for a new toothpaste. Name the toothpaste. Then plan a three-scene commercial. Include at least two pronouns in the description of each scene. Make sure that a reader would know what each pronoun refers to.

Name: ______________________________

Scene 1: ______________________________

____

____

____

____

Scene 2: ______________________________

____

____

____

____

Scene 3: ______________________________

____

____

____

____

Additional Practice: Using Pronouns

Using Contractions and Possessive Pronouns The following paragraph contains eight errors in the use of pronouns. Use proofreading marks to correct the paragraph. Then write a final draft.

If your going to take a vacation, Florida is a perfect state to visit. Its miles of coastline provide many opportunities for you're swimming, boating, and fishing fun. Florida also has an interesting history. It's origins can be seen in the style of many of the older buildings. Their red tile roofs and stucco walls are definitely Spanish. What's more, if your interested in tourist attractions, Florida has it's share, such as the Everglades. The people of Florida welcome tourists. Their ready to greet you and you're family any time with they're Southern hospitality.

Review: Using Pronouns

Using Pronouns Correctly Underline the correct pronouns in the sentences below.

1. Everyone told (her, their) side of the story.
2. The youth club just remodeled (its, it's) recreation room.
3. Ms. Sorkin gave Adam and (we, us) some tuna sandwiches.
4. Several brought (his, their) own equipment to the rock-climbing class.
5. At the corner the officer and (I, me) smiled at each other.
6. (Its, It's) very foggy along the coast this morning.
7. Few of the girls had cashed in (her, their) coupons.
8. Is everybody at (his, their) own house?
9. (We, Us) girls and (they, them) visited the greenhouse to see the azaleas.
10. (Their, They're) going to Texas this July to visit (their, they're) cousins.
11. It was (I, me) who called about the refund.
12. It was time for (we, us) swimmers to dress for the meet.
13. Tyler and Myra read (his or her, their) own stories to the class.
14. To (who, whom) do you think (your, you're) speaking?

Finding the Antecedents Underline each pronoun. Circle its antecedent and draw an arrow to it.

1. Giraffes get their supper from trees.
2. Juan understood the question. He answered it correctly.
3. The tree has lost its leaves. They are blowing all over the yard.
4. Tom made his famous chicken soup, and it was better than ever.
5. Delia handles her guitars carefully, since they are very valuable.
6. Tammy made some earrings. She gave them to her mom.
7. Angelo and Tina went fishing on several lakes in their canoe.
8. Carol made a huge sandwich and then ate it.

Skills Assessment 1 39

Handbooks 37–39

Directions One or more of the underlined sections in the following sentences may contain an error in grammar, usage, punctuation, spelling, or capitalization. Write the letter of each incorrect section. Then rewrite the section correctly. If there is no error in an item, write *E.*

Example You can type the word *typewriter.* By using only the top
A B
row of keys on the keyboard. No error
C D E
Answer A—*typewriter* by

1. The Nobel Prizes were established by Alfred Nobel, who invented
A B
dynamite, he also invented plywood. No error
C D E

2. Smokey the Bear's first name was Hot Foot Teddy. He warns you and I
A B C D
about forest fires. No error
E

3. An experiment with colored dishs of syrup has proved that bees can
A B C
distinguish colors. No error
D E

4. Belle Starr, known as the Bandit Queen, was married to Sam Starr. She
A B
and him were both horse thiefs. No error
C D E

5. Makers of tennis rackets have taken ounces off the weight of they're
A B C
products. By using lighter materials. No error
D E

6. We read *The Miracle Worker* in class, and some of we students acted
A B C
out different parts. Bernice and me took turns playing the role of
D
Anne Sullivan. No error
E

7. Womens' sports grow more important each year, and i find them fun
A B C D
to watch. No error
E

8. Bessie Smith, the greatest of the blues singers, often sang songs she
A B
wrote herself. No error
C D E

9. Did the magician really saw a woman in half. Its an incredible trick.
A B C D
No error
E

10. A favorite Korean dish is kimchi. It's a pickled vegetable seasoned with
A B C
garlic, pepper, and ginger. No error
D E

11. Rhode island and Maine have become popular vacation sites. Both of
A B C D
them were settled in the 1600s. No error
D E

12. Michael Jackson won three Grammy Awards in a single year for his
A B
recordings he has also starred in rock videoes. No error
C D E

13. Isn't this blank cassette your's? Perhaps it's mine, after all. No error
A B C D E

14. During the day some of the street musicians. Play his or her
A B
instruments near the train station. Angela and I enjoy listening to
C
them. No error
D E

15. Whom is a lions worst enemy? Hunters are. They have killed
A B C
thousands of lions. No error
D E

What Is a Verb?

A **verb** expresses an action, states that something exists, or links the subject in a sentence with a description of it. A sentence cannot exist without a verb.

The girl *jumped* over the first hurdle.
The class *thought* of a clever solution.

An **action verb** says what the subject of the sentence does.

Harold *painted* the fence. Miguel *studied* all weekend for the test.

A **linking verb** states that something exists, or is.

Ms. Davis *seems* friendly. This cat *is* a beautiful Persian.

Identifying Different Kinds of Verbs Underline the verb in each sentence. Then write *A* if the verb is an action verb or *L* if it is a linking verb.

_____ **1.** The Republic of Minerva is very small.

_____ **2.** It includes two coral reefs.

_____ **3.** The Pacific Ocean covers these coral reefs at high tide.

_____ **4.** Sealand is even tinier.

_____ **5.** It is the size of a baseball diamond.

_____ **6.** It lies in the English Channel.

_____ **7.** Beethoven's Fifth Symphony became the national anthem of the island nation of Morac-Songhrati-Meads.

_____ **8.** Two figs in a white star adorn the flag of that island nation.

_____ **9.** The national motto begins "Conscience, Intelligence, Courage."

_____ **10.** Meads Island, the capital of this country, is absent from most atlases.

_____ **11.** The oceans form a continuous mass of water on the earth's surface.

_____ **12.** Therefore, in a strict sense, the continents are islands.

_____ **13.** However, Greenland is really the largest island on the earth.

_____ **14.** Next in size comes New Guinea.

_____ **15.** Sometimes a volcano makes a new island in the sea.

_____ **16.** The Hawaiian Islands began that way.

_____ **17.** Millions of people live on islands like Japan and the Philippines.

_____ **18.** Other islands have no people at all.

_____ **19.** Pelican Island in Florida is an example.

_____ **20.** Imagine the island of California!

Verbs and Direct Objects

The **direct object** is the noun or pronoun that receives the action of the verb. To find the direct object in a sentence, ask *what* or *whom* after the verb.

The dog chewed my *slippers.* (Chewed what? *slippers*)
Jan carried a *hairbrush* in her bag. (Carried what? *hairbrush*)
I saw *Ernie* crossing the street. (Saw whom? *Ernie*)
Our class sent *volunteers* to Children's Hospital.
(Sent whom? *volunteers*)

Identifying Verbs and Direct Objects Put one line under each verb and two lines under each direct object.

1. Underline the verb in each of these sentences.
2. The falling snow quickly covered our tracks.
3. Pour the hot wax into the candle mold.
4. Some gardeners fertilize their flowers with fish meal.
5. The spider spun its web between two branches.
6. The Emancipation Proclamation abolished slavery in the Confederacy.
7. Lincoln issued his proclamation on January 1, 1863.
8. The early Egyptians loved emeralds.
9. The planet Mars has a thin atmosphere.
10. We saw the Suez Canal from the air.

Using Direct Objects Add direct objects to the following sentences.

1. Matt read the ______________________.
2. Lee practices the ______________________ for an hour every day.
3. The fire severely damaged the ______________________.
4. We need ______________________ to make this world a better place.
5. Susan built a(n) ______________________ based on her own design.
6. Everyone followed the ______________________ down the trail.
7. Ramona saw two ______________________.
8. Please bring your ______________________ to school today.

Transitive and Intransitive Verbs

When a word in a sentence answers the question *whom* or *what* after the verb, that word is a *direct object.*

A verb that has a direct object is called a **transitive verb**.

Joan *moved* the lamp. (transitive verb)

A verb that does not have a direct object is called an **intransitive verb**.

Joan *moved* to Ohio. (intransitive verb)

Identifying Transitive and Intransitive Verbs In the following sentences, underline each verb. Then write *T* if the verb is transitive or *I* if the verb is intransitive. Put a double line under the direct object if there is one.

_____ **1.** Many carpenters build their own toolboxes.

_____ **2.** We divided these suggestions into four categories.

_____ **3.** The monkeys peered through the bars of their cages.

_____ **4.** Some boys grew restless during the long ceremony.

_____ **5.** The tide rises quickly on this part of the coast.

_____ **6.** This morning the dentist put fluoride on my teeth.

_____ **7.** Set the table for eight people.

_____ **8.** The river overflowed several times that spring.

_____ **9.** Patrick Henry spoke eloquently.

_____ **10.** Louise and Juanita made several clever posters for the dance.

_____ **11.** The captain expertly guided his ship past the rocks.

_____ **12.** Their quarterback was just too quick for us.

_____ **13.** We all drank our lemonade slowly during the long, hot afternoon.

_____ **14.** Even at a distance he smelled the overripe bananas.

_____ **15.** Jill looks pretty good in her new glasses.

_____ **16.** A stitch in time saves nine.

_____ **17.** The farmer helped the calf to its feet.

_____ **18.** Jaguars range from the southwestern United States to Argentina.

_____ **19.** Martin Luther King, Jr., won a Nobel Prize in 1964.

_____ **20.** Close to the horizon, the moon looks larger.

Linking Verbs and Predicate Words

A **linking verb** connects, or links, the subject of the sentence with the **predicate word,** a word in the predicate that modifies the subject. Some linking verbs are *am, is, are, was, were, be, seem, look, appear, smell, taste, feel, sound, remain, grow,* and *become.* Linking verbs do not have direct objects.

Linking Verb The boy *is* an artist. (*Artist* is linked to *boy.*)
Joyce *sounded* unconcerned.
(*Unconcerned* describes *Joyce.*)

Transitive Verb Cheryl *sounded* the alarm. (*Alarm* is the direct object.)

Identifying Linking Verbs Underline the subject once and the linking verb twice. Then draw a circle around the predicate word.

Example The woman in the next room is a well-known (poet.)

1. Temperatures remain steady in the coastal areas.
2. The first Ford automobiles were always black.
3. After the marathon Henry felt weak and tired.
4. In 1993 Bill Clinton became the nation's forty-second president.
5. Smoking is hazardous to everyone's health.
6. Our weather grew more humid this year.
7. That band sounds terrible to me.
8. Something about the situation looked strange to the sheriff.
9. The last minutes of the game seemed endless.
10. The air smells sweet in spring.

Identifying Linking Verbs and Transitive Verbs In each sentence, underline the verb. On the line, write *L* if the verb is linking or *T* if the verb is transitive.

_____ 1. That Winesap apple was really good.

_____ 2. Without hesitation, the sergeant pulled the alarm.

_____ 3. This year gymnastics became my favorite sport.

_____ 4. She carefully sanded the rough edges of the wood.

_____ 5. The boxer appeared groggy after the third round.

_____ 6. Laura sounded excited about her summer job.

Verb Phrases

A **verb phrase** consists of a **main verb** and one or more **helping verbs.** Some common helping verbs are forms of *be, have,* and *do.* Here are some additional helping verbs:

will go	*can* go	*would* go	*could* go	*must* go
shall go	*may* go	*should* go	*might* go	

The words that make up a verb phrase are sometimes separated by other words that are not verbs.

should not *have gone*	*will* probably *arrive*
might never *have happened*	*could* barely *understand*

Identifying Parts of the Verb Write *HV* over the helping verbs and *MV* over the main verbs in the following sentences.

Example Brett might (HV) have (HV) gone (MV) to the movies.

1. Venus will be close to the Moon this evening.
2. Jane could never finish a whole sandwich at once.
3. The pendulum on the old clock may have been repaired.
4. Does a new broom sweep clean?
5. Brad should have been studying for that test.
6. Have you ever seen a cranberry bog?
7. The next batter will probably hit the ball out of the park.
8. Why don't you run for student council president?

Using Helping Verbs The following sentences have main verbs but no helping verbs. Write helping verbs on the lines.

1. We ________________ never see such a sight again.
2. You ________________ always check your work carefully.
3. She ________________ often call me after dinner.
4. ________________ you throw the ball hard?
5. ________________ you made your costume yet?
6. I ________________ finish this project tonight, or it will be late.

Tenses of Verbs

Different forms of a verb are used to show the time of an action or a state of being. These forms are called the **tenses** of the verb.

Tense changes are made in three ways:

1. By a change in the ending: *talk, talked*
2. By a change in the spelling: *ring, rang, rung*
3. By a change in the helping verbs: *has talked, will talk*

Here are five important tenses:

Present Tense	she calls	we speak
Future Tense	she will call	we shall speak
Past Tense	she called	we spoke
Present Perfect Tense	she has called	we have spoken
Past Perfect Tense	she had called	we had spoken

Identifying Tenses Underline the verb in each sentence. Write its tense on the line at the right.

1. Carbon dioxide is soluble in water. ____________
2. We hiked in the Grand Canyon last summer. ____________
3. Write me a letter. ____________
4. Have you read any poems by E. E. Cummings? ____________
5. Debby will light the candles tonight. ____________
6. Earlier I had opened the kitchen window. ____________
7. All week the choir practiced for the concert. ____________
8. Had you ever heard that song before? ____________

Using Tenses Write the correct form of the verb for each sentence.

Example Matthew (present perfect of *go*) to work. has gone

1. Toshi (past of *write*) a long letter. ____________
2. Bonita (future of *graduate*) in June. ____________
3. Barb (present perfect of *learn*) the trick easily. ____________
4. Greg (past perfect of *see*) the film four times. ____________
5. The home team (present of *win*) regularly. ____________

Principal Parts: Regular Verbs

Verb tenses are made by using the three **principal parts** of verbs: the **present**, the **past**, and the **past participle.** If you know the principal parts of a verb, you can make any tense by using the forms alone or with helping verbs.

Remember these two rules when you are forming verbs:

1. **The past form of the verb is used alone, without a helping verb.**
2. **The past participle is used with a helping verb.**

Most English verbs are **regular**. The past form of a regular verb is made by adding *-ed* or *-d* to the present. The past participle is the same as the past but is used with a helping verb. Note that the spelling of some regular verbs changes when *-d* or *-ed* is added.

Present	Past	Past Participle	Present	Past	Past Participle
join	joined	(have) joined	carry	carried	(have) carried
like	liked	(have) liked	trap	trapped	(have) trapped

Identifying the Principal Parts of Regular Verbs Write the principal parts of the following regular verbs.

	Present	Past	Past Participle
1. jump	____________	____________	____________
2. push	____________	____________	____________
3. love	____________	____________	____________
4. move	____________	____________	____________
5. shape	____________	____________	____________
6. tap	____________	____________	____________
7. fix	____________	____________	____________
8. watch	____________	____________	____________
9. erase	____________	____________	____________
10. kick	____________	____________	____________
11. carry	____________	____________	____________
12. like	____________	____________	____________

Irregular Verbs (I)

Verbs that do not follow the regular pattern of adding *-d* or *-ed* to the present to form the past and past participle are called **irregular verbs.**

For some irregular verbs, the past and the past participle forms are spelled the same. Often, the past and the past participle are not the same.

Here are the principal parts of four common irregular verbs.

Present	Past	Past Participle
begin	began	(have) begun
break	broke	(have) broken
bring	brought	(have) brought
choose	chose	(have) chosen

Using Irregular Verbs Underline the correct forms of the irregular verbs in parentheses.

1. No one is sure when language (began, begun) in the human species.
2. Robert has (chose, chosen) to study Italian as well as English.
3. Finally the huge truck was (brought, brung) to a halt.
4. People dislike politicians who have (broke, broken) their promises.
5. Ernest Hemingway was (chose, chosen) for a Nobel Prize in 1954.
6. Several more records in track have been (broke, broken) this year.
7. Amiko had (began, begun) her reading with Mother Goose rhymes.
8. Often, hard times have (bring, brought) out the best in people.
9. Because spring was early, the fruit trees (began, begun) to bloom.
10. You could not have (chose, chosen) a more interesting project.
11. Unfortunately, that jar of sorghum in my backpack (broke, broken).
12. African slaves were (bring, brought) to Portugal as early as 1440.
13. The voters (chose, chosen) a candidate nobody had expected to win.
14. Sarah (began, begun) to wonder what her dream might mean.
15. Graffiti covered the walls, and several windows were (broke, broken).
16. Fresh forces were (brought, brung) in by the Confederate general.

Irregular Verbs (II)

Here are the principal parts of four more irregular verbs.

Present	Past	Past Participle
come	came	(have) come
do	did	(have) done
drink	drank	(have) drunk
eat	ate	(have) eaten

Using Irregular Verbs Underline the correct forms of the irregular verbs in parentheses.

1. A dreadful tyrant has (came, come) to a bad end.
2. The dog jumped up on the counter and (ate, eaten) half the birthday cake.
3. Isaac Newton (did, done) some important research in optics.
4. The camel originally (came, come) from North America, and from there it migrated to Asia.
5. Rust had (ate, eaten) into the iron hull of the great ship.
6. Every evening the animals (drank, drunk) from the nearby stream.
7. Jill had (came, come) into a small inheritance when her aunt died.
8. Until his arrest, the embezzler thought he had (did, done) nothing that would arouse suspicion.
9. When I had the flu, I (drank, drunk) as much fruit juice as I could.
10. Have you ever (ate, eaten) fried okra that tasted as good as this?
11. We were wondering why the mail carrier (came, come) to our house so early in the day.
12. Have you ever (drank, drunk) goat's milk?
13. The winter (did, done) severe damage to the highways in this state.
14. For six days, until their rescue, the miners (ate, eaten) nothing but some stale sandwiches.
15. Investigating the crime, Sherlock Holmes set out to discover who had (did, done) it.
16. The baby has (drank, drunk) more milk than usual today.

Irregular Verbs (III)

Here are the principal parts of four more irregular verbs.

Present	Past	Past Participle
fall	fell	(have) fallen
freeze	froze	(have) frozen
give	gave	(have) given
go	went	(have) gone

Using Irregular Verbs Underline the correct forms of the irregular verbs in parentheses.

1. Their hopes had (fell, fallen) when the sailboat failed to return at daybreak.
2. We all should have (went, gone) to that drama club meeting yesterday.
3. The woman's smile (froze, frozen) upon her face.
4. I think you should have (gave, given) the waitress a larger tip.
5. Our family (gone, went) on a vacation to New England.
6. Christmas (fell, fallen) on a Saturday in 1993.
7. The ferns were (froze, frozen) in the ice.
8. The break in the weather (gave, given) us a chance to get the crops in after all.
9. A star (fell, fallen) last night.
10. We couldn't go skating yet because the pond had not (froze, frozen) over completely.
11. Andrés has (went, gone) swimming at the public pool every day this summer.
12. In some cities the police have been (gave, given) bulletproof vests.
13. Clara (went, gone) for the doctor in plenty of time.
14. By the early 1930s, the United States had (fell, fallen) into an economic depression.
15. The jinni (gave, given) Aladdin three wishes.
16. Waiting so long for the bus, I thought my toes were (froze, frozen).

Irregular Verbs (IV)

Here are the principal parts of four more irregular verbs.

Present	Past	Past Participle
grow	grew	(have) grown
know	knew	(have) known
ride	rode	(have) ridden
ring	rang	(have) rung

Using Irregular Verbs Underline the correct forms of the irregular verbs in parentheses.

1. My mother's family (grew, grown) beans in Indiana.
2. Regina has (knew, known) how to swim since she was three years old.
3. Has Lin ever (rode, ridden) on the roller coaster?
4. Even in ancient times, some people (knew, known) that the earth is round.
5. The church bells (rang, rung) out loudly in the village square.
6. The audience had (grew, grown) quite restless by the time the curtain finally rose.
7. Lucia (rode, ridden) a horse as if she had been born on it.
8. I might have (rang, rung) the doorbell, but I decided to knock instead.
9. Mark (grew, grown) a few inches last year.
10. If I had (knew, known) then what I learned later, things might have worked out differently.
11. Late one night a shrill scream (rang, rung) out in the dark courtyard below.
12. Side by side, we (rode, ridden) along in silence.
13. One of your ideas has really (rang, rung) a bell with me.
14. When the dust cleared, they saw that the outlaws had (rode, ridden) away.
15. By then the citizens had (grew, grown) quite tired of the gunfire.
16. Only one person (knew, known) who the culprit really was.

Irregular Verbs (V)

Here are the principal parts of four more irregular verbs.

Present	Past	Past Participle
run	ran	(have) run
see	saw	(have) seen
sing	sang	(have) sung
speak	spoke	(have) spoken

Using Irregular Verbs Underline the correct forms of the irregular verbs in parentheses.

1. At least seventeen people have now (ran, run) the mile in less than four minutes.
2. Halley's comet was last (saw, seen) in 1986.
3. Kathryn (sang, sung) several Irish folk tunes in her recital.
4. Your friends (spoke, spoken) well of you when I saw them.
5. We (saw, seen) at once that the room had been disturbed.
6. Chinese is (spoke, spoken) by more people than any other language in the world.
7. I wanted to write you a letter yesterday, but I (ran, run) out of time.
8. The chorus (sang, sung) in the last movement of Beethoven's Ninth Symphony.
9. When Sheri was in Kenya, she (spoke, spoken) the Swahili language.
10. A consumer magazine (ran, run) several tests on CD players.
11. When the last notes had been (sang, sung), the audience erupted in applause.
12. I haven't (saw, seen) the northern lights since I lived in Canada.
13. Some of the tales were written down, but most were only (spoke, spoken).
14. According to the accident report, the plane had (ran, run) out of gas.
15. Woody Guthrie had (sang, sung) his songs all over the country.
16. We thought we (saw, seen) the light at the end of the tunnel.

Irregular Verbs (VI)

Here are the principal parts of four more irregular verbs.

Present	Past	Past Participle
steal	stole	(have) stolen
take	took	(have) taken
throw	threw	(have) thrown
write	wrote	(have) written

Using Irregular Verbs Underline the correct forms of the irregular verbs in parentheses.

1. Michelle has (stole, stolen) more bases than anybody else on our team.

2. She (took, taken) a chance in today's game, and it really paid off.

3. The fielder (threw, thrown) the ball well, but not well enough.

4. Until now, I had (wrote, written) off our team's chances this year.

5. The proud father (stole, stolen) a look at his sleeping baby.

6. We (took, taken) advantage of the fine spring day to try out our new kite design.

7. Hasn't World War II been (wrote, written) about a great deal?

8. When the gyroscope failed, the ship was (threw, thrown) completely off its course.

9. Several planes have (took, taken) off to aid the rescue mission.

10. The senator (threw, thrown) a big party after she won the election.

11. William Shakespeare (wrote, written) some beautiful sonnets in addition to his plays.

12. The fox (stole, stolen) softly into the chicken coop.

13. By the end of the month, he will have (took, taken) both his written exam and his road test.

14. A world-famous painting was (stole, stolen) from a European museum.

15. Several newspapers (wrote, written) long stories about it.

16. The thieves had (threw, thrown) a smoke bomb to aid their escape.

Irregular Verbs (VII)

Using Irregular Verbs Underline the correct forms of the irregular verbs in parentheses.

1. Romeo and Juliet had (fell, fallen) in love despite their families' feud.
2. Shakespeare's play about those lovers was (wrote, written) in 1594.
3. The popularity of the play (grew, grown) over the years.
4. Many a performer has (spoke, spoken) those famous lines.
5. Our class (saw, seen) the play performed at the high school.
6. Some think Shakespeare (began, begun) his career as a schoolteacher.
7. Sailors once believed that mermaids (sang, sung) to them at sea.
8. According to legend, sea serpents have also (rode, ridden) the waves.
9. Many who have (went, gone) to sea have heard these strange old tales.
10. Sailors of old (knew, known) much danger and hardship.
11. They (brung, brought) their fears and dreams aboard ship with them.
12. Sometimes, after they (did, done) their chores, they sang songs and told stories.
13. Our water pipes were (froze, frozen) during that cold snap last week.
14. The snowfall (broke, broken) the local record.
15. We lost our electricity, and several large old trees were (threw, thrown) down by heavy winds.
16. After a while we nearly (ran, run) out of fuel.
17. To top it off, someone had (stole, stolen) our snow shovel.
18. When our telephone (rang, rung), we knew we were not totally isolated.
19. A month from now, I hope spring will have (came, come).
20. Today we all (took, taken) out our skis and sleds and went out to have some fun in the snow.
21. We (chose, chosen) up sides for some games.
22. Then we came in and (drank, drunk) hot cocoa.
23. I was so hungry I could have (ate, eaten) a horse or two.
24. The experience (gave, given) me a chance to find out about having fun without TV.

Choosing the Right Verb: Let *and* Leave

Let means "to allow" or "to permit."

> *Let* her stay for a while.
> David *lets* me use his bike.

Leave means "to depart" or "to let stay or be."

> *Leave* the room.
> They will *leave* the books on the table.

The principal parts of these verbs are as follows:

> let, let, let   leave, left, left

Choosing the Right Verb Underline the correct words in parentheses.

1. Don't (let, leave) your camera in a hot place for too long.
2. You had better (let, leave) the traffic clear before you try to get across this highway.
3. Marie Antoinette supposedly said, "(Let, Leave) them eat cake."
4. Do you (let, leave) your cat go out of the house in this neighborhood?
5. Do you (let, leave) him out all night?
6. Please (let, leave) me alone so that I can get some work done.
7. (Let, Leave) the water seek its own level.
8. We should (let, leave) the sails in the sun long enough for them to dry.
9. The rangers decided to (let, leave) the fire burn itself out.
10. The guards waited for the shoplifter to (let, leave) the store.
11. When he is caught, they will not soon (let, leave) him go.
12. When we redecorate, I think it would be nice to (let, leave) the old wallpaper in this room.
13. At least (let, leave) it stay on the south wall.
14. This new race car will (let, leave) the rest of them in the dust.
15. You'd better not (let, leave) it out of your sight.
16. "(Let, Leave) the buyer beware," the old saying goes.
17. Another one is "(Let, Leave) the chips fall where they may."
18. It is wise to (let, leave) enough space for a new tree to grow where the other one stood.
19. Please (let, leave) me explain what really happened.
20. You (let, leave) me no alternative but to tell the truth.

Choosing the Right Verb: Lie *and* Lay

Lie means "to rest" or "to recline." It does not take an object.
Lay means "to put or place." It takes an object.

The principal parts of these verbs are as follows:

lie, lay, lain   lay, laid, laid

Choosing the Right Verb Underline the correct words in parentheses.

1. Immigrant workers (lay, laid) the railroad tracks that crossed the United States.
2. As we speak, curious treasures (lie, lay) hidden at the bottom of the sea.
3. It is best to let sleeping dogs (lie, lay).
4. Be not the first by whom the new is tried, nor yet the last to (lie, lay) the old aside.
5. I (lay, laid) awake for a long time, listening to the storm.
6. We hope the old hen will (lie, lay) an egg today.
7. When the trainer gives a signal, the dog will (lie, lay) down on the grass.
8. Let us (lie, lay) all our cards on the table.
9. He just wants to (lie, lay) around in his room all day long.
10. He (lay, laid) around yesterday.
11. He has (lain, laid) around all week.
12. The bricklayer has (lain, laid) an amazing number of bricks today.
13. You'd better (lie, lay) on the sofa awhile until you feel better.
14. The reporter (lay, laid) her briefcase down on a chair in the courtroom.
15. We (lay, laid) some keepsakes in the old strongbox.
16. A lovely old pearl (lay, lain) at the bottom of the drawer.
17. The turtle will probably (lie, lay) on that rock in the sun all day long.
18. The wallet had (lay, lain) there unnoticed for nearly an hour.
19. When the old man had been (lain, laid) to rest, the mourners left.
20. The sheriff told her to (lie, lay) that pistol down.
21. (Lay, Lie) the mechanic's tools in that metal box.
22. I (lay, laid) my keys down somewhere, and now I can't find them.

Choosing the Right Verb: Sit and Set

Sit means "to be in a seat" or "to rest." It does not take an object.

Sat is the past of *sit.* It means "was seated" or "was rested." Since *sat* is a form of *sit,* it does not take an object.

Set is a different word entirely. It means "to put or place." It takes an object.

The principal parts of these verbs are as follows:

sit, sat, sat   set, set, set

Choosing the Right Verb Underline the correct words in parentheses.

1. Throughout the game we had to (sit, set) in the end zone.
2. Those old magazines have (sat, set) on the table for months.
3. Why don't you (sit, set) down your load and rest awhile?
4. Who (sat, set) the record for the discus throw in the Olympics?
5. How long do you suppose this plane will (sit, set) on the runway?
6. We'll have to (sit, set) a limit on spending next year.
7. For a long time Adam has (sat, set) quietly, putting his model plane together.
8. The old clock has (sat, set) on that ledge for a long time.
9. Sometimes it's hard for children to (sit, set) still long enough to have their picture taken.
10. (Sit, Set) the photograph up on the shelf where we all can see it.
11. Has your sister (sat, set) a date for her wedding?
12. We'll need to (sit, set) up more chairs on the lawn.
13. The French students who are visiting us will (sit, set) in the front row of the theater.
14. I've (sat, set) here an hour waiting for you.
15. Your boots are (sitting, setting) there, exactly where you left them.
16. (Sit, Set) aside whatever doubts you may have.
17. They've been (sitting, setting) up a new exhibit at the space museum.
18. There the army (sat, set), waiting for reinforcements.
19. My friends were (sitting, setting) around, wondering what to do.
20. They (sat, set) there for another hour and then went home.
21. I had (sat, set) my watch for a different time zone.
22. Sometimes forests are (sat, set) on fire by lightning.

Linking Grammar and Writing: Using Verbs

Your class has decided to prepare a baby-sitting handbook. Picture yourself as a member of the committee chosen to direct this project. Your job is to review the suggestions submitted by the class. Below are five of these suggestions. Rewrite them, correcting any errors in the use of verbs. Mark the ideas that you think should not be included in the handbook. Then add three ideas of your own.

1. When you set with young children, you shouldn't let them alone.
2. You can lay down on the couch, especially if it gets late.
3. If a child has already ate, be sure to check with his or her parents about snacks.
4. Once a little boy had hid the house key. We was outside and had to climbed in the window.
5. Usually I brought a list of emergency phone numbers, just in case my clients forget to leave them.

1. ____

____

2. ____

____

3. ____

____

4. ____

____

5. ____

____

____

____

____

____

____

Additional Practice: Using Verbs

Analyzing Linking Verbs and Action Verbs Underline the verbs in the following sentences. For each linking verb, draw an arrow from the predicate word back to the word it is linked to. For each action verb, draw an arrow from the verb to its direct object, if there is one.

Example Jan seems cheerful today.

1. In the old days in Chicago, you could smell the stockyards miles away.
2. The clothes smelled really fresh after hanging outside all afternoon.
3. The park looked somewhat eerie after dark.
4. The defendant looked nervously around the courtroom.
5. You should taste this stew before serving it.
6. Does it taste too peppery?
7. They will sound the alarm in case of an extremely high tide.
8. Her name sounds very familiar.
9. The magician finally appeared upon the stage.
10. After a few minutes, the audience appeared completely fascinated by him.

Using Verbs Correctly Underline the correct verbs in parentheses.

1. Now that the pond has (froze, frozen) solid, we can go ice-skating.
2. The pony (drank, drunk) a whole bucket of water.
3. Neil just (come, came) home from college yesterday.
4. I should have (wrote, written) sooner about our vacation plans.
5. (Let, Leave) the dog alone when it is eating.
6. Anna has (broke, broken) the lock on her bicycle chain.
7. During the crisis Harold (did, done) what he was asked.
8. The choir had never (sang, sung) that piece before.

Review: Using Verbs

Identifying Transitive and Intransitive Verbs Find the verb in each of the following sentences. If the verb is transitive, underline it and circle its direct object. If the verb is intransitive, just underline it.

Example The girl has <u>bought</u> a (scarf.) The girl <u>is</u> very pretty.

1. A stumble may prevent a fall.
2. Recently astronomers have observed some extremely distant galaxies.
3. Our sunflowers have grown very tall this year.
4. Justice to others is charity for ourselves.
5. Were you ready for this exercise?

Identifying the Tenses Underline the verb in each sentence. Then name the tense on the line. The five tenses used are *present, future, past, present perfect,* and *past perfect.*

1. Have you written to your cousins lately? ____________________
2. Sadie's Siamese cat sits quietly by the window. ____________________
3. I met a traveler from an antique land. ____________________
4. When shall we see an eclipse of the sun? ____________________
5. We had eaten all the salad before the party. ____________________

Using Verbs Correctly Underline the correct verbs in parentheses.

1. Have you (chose, chosen) your favorite song on this album?
2. "Someone has (drank, drunk) all my milk," said the little bear.
3. Luiz has (gave, given) me a book about unidentified flying objects.
4. Clare has never (went, gone) tobogganing before.
5. Yesterday I (ran, run) three miles in twenty minutes.
6. On his way home, Chuck (saw, seen) a terrible accident.
7. He had never (saw, seen) so many emergency vehicles.
8. Beth has (wrote, written) a letter to the editor of the magazine.
9. You should have (come, came) to the student-government meeting.
10. Michiko has (grew, grown) a little taller over the summer.

What Is an Adjective?

An **adjective** is a word that modifies a noun or a pronoun. A **proper adjective** is made from a proper noun and begins with a capital letter. *Hawaiian* and *Victorian* are proper adjectives.

Adjectives help give your reader a clear picture of what you are talking about. They limit, or modify, the meaning of the word.

1. *What kind: yellow* ribbon, *cold* nose, *Irish* music
2. *How much or how many: seven* dwarfs, *some* people, *less* juice
3. *Which one or ones: this* glove, *that* pirate, *these* cameras

Finding the Adjectives Underline the adjectives in each of the following sentences. (You need not include *a, an,* or *the.*) Circle the proper adjectives.

1. Sculptures have been made from many different materials.

2. The first sculptors used bone and ivory.

3. Greek sculptors carved huge marble blocks into human forms.

4. The ancient Greeks also made colossal bronze statues.

5. African masks have been sculpted from wood.

6. At Mount Rushmore, a magnificent sculpture of four presidential faces has been cut into a craggy mountain.

7. One artist piled rocks in a lake and called the arrangement a modern masterpiece.

8. A French chef in New York chisels ice sculptures.

9. Machine parts are used to form mechanical sculptures.

10. Even neon lights have been used to create artworks.

Using Adjectives Write one or more clear, exact adjectives on each line.

1. The ________________ car is clean.

2. The ________________ baker gave us ________________ rolls.

3. ________________ people like ________________ music.

4. A ________________ gorilla walked into the ________________ cage.

5. The ________________ woman carried the ________________ box.

6. The ________________ men ate their food.

Predicate Adjectives

Adjectives usually come before the words they modify.

The *old* and *tattered* doll lay at the bottom of the trunk.

Sometimes they are put after the words they modify.

The doll, *old* and *tattered,* lay at the bottom of the trunk.

In some sentences, however, adjectives are separated from the words they modify by linking verbs. These adjectives are called predicate adjectives because they appear in the predicate.

A **predicate adjective** is an adjective that follows a linking verb. It describes the subject of the sentence.

S LV PA
The day was sunny. (*Sunny* modifies *day.*)

Finding Linking Verbs and Predicate Adjectives In the following sentences, underline the subjects once and the linking verbs twice. Then circle the predicate adjectives. There might be more than one predicate adjective in a sentence.

Example The assignment seemed easy.

1. In the morning light, the house looked drab and dingy.

2. Gary's shoulders felt sore for several days.

3. At the end of the race, the runner looked sweaty but joyful.

4. The forest appeared silver in the moonlight.

5. I felt uncomfortable on the first day of school.

6. As we approach, the volcano seems gigantic.

7. The woods smell fresh and earthy in springtime.

8. The voice on the phone sounded quite strange.

9. The weather has turned rather cold this week.

10. The timbers of the old barn have become weathered and worn.

11. Some people grow older but not wiser.

12. In this rain, the path seems even longer than usual.

13. Aren't your parents happy about the news?

14. Our neighbor's peaches tasted sweet and juicy.

15. Something about the situation didn't look right.

16. Isn't this room cozy?

Adjectives in Comparisons

Adjectives can be used to compare one thing with another, or one thing with many other things.

Jupiter is *bigger* than Saturn.
Jupiter is the *biggest* of the planets.

Use the comparative form of an adjective to compare two things. Form the comparative by adding *-er* to the adjective.

big + -er = bigger

Use the superlative form of an adjective to compare three or more things. Form the superlative by adding *-est* to the adjective.

big + -est = biggest

For adjectives ending in *y,* change the *y* to *i* before adding *-er* or *-est.*

easy easier easiest

Longer adjectives use *more* for the comparative form and *most* for the superlative form.

Adjective	Comparative Form	Superlative Form
beautiful	more beautiful	most beautiful
special	more special	most special

A few adjectives have different words as their comparative and superlative forms.

good	better	best
bad	worse	worst

Using Adjectives in Comparison Write the correct form of each adjective.

1. Your shoes look (comparative of *new*) than mine. ____________
2. Our team is the (superlative of *good*). ____________
3. That test was the (superlative of *difficult*). ____________
4. Susan seemed (comparative of *happy*) than Pat. ____________
5. Of the two towels, this one feels (comparative of *soft*). ____________
6. This puppy is the (superlative of *small*) of the litter. ____________
7. My cold got (comparative of *bad*). ____________
8. Mr. Roper was (comparative of *cranky*) than usual. ____________
9. Everybody seemed (comparative of *silent*) than usual. ____________
10. It was the (superlative of *long*) night of my life. ____________

Possessive Pronouns Used as Adjectives

A possessive pronoun sometimes modifies a noun. Then it is considered an adjective that answers the question *which one* or *which ones* about the noun. When used with a noun, a possessive pronoun helps make the meaning of the noun more definite.

my locker *your* boots *their* desks

Your, my, her, his, our, its, and *their* are possessive pronouns used as adjectives.

Finding Pronouns Used as Adjectives Underline each possessive pronoun. Then draw an arrow from the possessive pronoun to the word it modifies.

Example The dog buried <u>its</u> bone in <u>our</u> front garden.

1. Pablo played us a tune on his panpipe.
2. The old house had lost its shingles during our last big storm.
3. Did you answer his question correctly?
4. Your wish is my command.
5. This lawn mower is old, and its blades are quite rusty.
6. The squirrel was frightened by my sudden appearance.
7. Recently my father visited his old high school friend.
8. Inuit people build their igloos from snow.
9. Our research topic was the Great Barrier Reef.
10. Several giraffes extended their long necks over the fence.
11. This month our dentist changed her appointment schedule.
12. Have you made up your mind about my offer?
13. Her brother was also her best friend.
14. Their improvements in the house had increased its value.
15. Please give my sincere apologies to your aunt.

Demonstrative Adjective or Demonstrative Pronoun?

The words *this, that, these,* and *those* may be used as modifiers with nouns or pronouns to point out specific persons or things. When used as modifiers, these four words are called **demonstrative adjectives**. They tell *which one* or which ones about the words they modify.

I like *this* coat, but I don't like *that* one.

When used by themselves, these words are called **demonstrative pronouns.**

I don't like *that.* *This* is better.

As adjectives, *this* and *that* are used with singular nouns. *These* and *those* are used with plural nouns.

The nouns *kind* and *sort* are singular. We say *this kind* and *this sort. These kinds* and *those sorts* are plural.

Finding the Demonstrative Adjectives and Pronouns Underline each demonstrative adjective once. Underline each demonstrative pronoun twice.

1. That arrow in the weather vane points east.
2. Do you like those kittens, or do you prefer these?
3. This album is Karen's favorite. Think of that!
4. I find these kinds of pets more appealing and that's the important thing.
5. These are the rules for the debate.

Using Demonstrative Adjectives On each line, write *this kind, that kind, that sort, these sorts,* or *those kinds.* Check that all the words are singular or that all the words are plural.

1. We will use less electricity with ____________________ of appliances.
2. ____________________ of parties always take time to plan.
3. ____________________ of mystery story makes me shiver.
4. I don't like ____________________ of jokes.
5. Please find me ____________________ of pen.
6. ____________________ of roller coaster is especially exciting.
7. ____________________ of records are difficult to find.
8. Can I buy ____________________ of fishhook in this store?

Linking Grammar and Writing: Using Adjectives

One type of poem is a list of descriptive phrases, each made up of an adjective and a noun. The final line of the poem names the subject. For example:

Tremendous strength
Massive jaw
Defiant roar
Long climb
Furious stare
King Kong

On the lines below, write two poems that follow this pattern. Choose specific subjects, such as "deputy sheriff," "roller rink," or "giant redwood." Try to use colorful adjectives.

Imagine that you have just arrived at your favorite vacation spot. Write a postcard telling a friend back home about the great time you are having. Include several adjectives and underline them. Include at least two predicate adjectives and two pronouns used as adjectives. Follow good letter form.

Additional Practice: Using Adjectives

Finding Adjectives Underline all of the adjectives in these sentences. Include predicate adjectives, demonstrative adjectives, and articles.

1. Maria carefully wrapped the French bread in some heavy foil.
2. That popular star receives more letters in one day than I do in five years.
3. The antique wooden trunk had large hinges.
4. These African violets thrive in direct sunlight.
5. The older cabins are cold and dirty.
6. This American car gets better mileage than most foreign imports.
7. Are these beautiful watches Swiss?
8. The landlord replaced that old worn carpeting in the front lobby.

Using Adjectives Correctly Rewrite these sentences, correcting any errors in the use of adjectives.

1. This coat is the warmer of the three, and it feels the coziest.

   ____

2. This lake looks more cleaner than the other, but it's farthest from our house.

   ____

3. These sort of clothing is comfortabler in the summer.

   ____

4. What is the worse thing that ever happened to you?

   ____

5. Of the two dogs, this one is most friendliest.

   ____

6. My watch is accurater than yours, and it's prettiest too.

   ____

7. Which state has the most warmest weather in the whole country?

   ____

8. I don't care for those kind of movie.

   ____

Review: Using Adjectives

Identifying Adjectives Underline each word used as an adjective in the sentences below. Circle the modified word, and draw an arrow to it. Ignore *a, an,* and *the.*

1. Many brave explorers crossed the snowy tundra.
2. Her curly hair appeared shinier in the noonday sun.
3. This lovely Japanese kimono is made of blue silk.
4. The rowdy, irresponsible audience ruined that fine show.
5. A mysterious stranger sauntered up to that bossy clerk.
6. This morning our newest student was shy.
7. It was a cold February, and an icy fog hung in the dirty air.
8. In the midst of the confusion, the little girl felt confident.

Recognizing Possessive Pronouns Underline the possessive pronouns in the following sentences. Draw an arrow from each pronoun to the word it modifies.

1. Waiting for their father, Rachel and Sarah saw his car in the distance.
2. My favorite puppy followed its mother into our kitchen.
3. Daniel took his skateboard outside and painted its top.
4. The flowers in our window box are opening their buds.
5. Raul's aunt gave him her old radio.
6. Your guess is as good as Kenneth's.
7. Maria put her skis together and pointed their tips downhill.
8. Toni and I remembered to bring our snorkels to your pool.

What Is an Adverb?

An **adverb** modifies a verb, an adjective, or another adverb.

We walked *slowly.* (adverb modifying verb)

The sky was *fairly* clear. (adverb modifying adjective)

Joe talked *rather* quietly. (adverb modifying another adverb)

Adverbs tell *how, when, where,* or *to what extent.*

Finding the Adverbs Underline each adverb. Draw an arrow from the adverb to the word it modifies. Watch for double adverbs.

Example We did our chores more quickly today.

1. A load of salmon arrived on the docks today.

2. The guard walked very cautiously into the building.

3. Our space probe landed softly on the moon yesterday.

4. The lifeguard swam extremely fast.

5. Quickly, we gathered our gear and prepared to leave soon.

6. The busy beaver gnawed quite furiously on the tree trunk.

7. I am well pleased with my new job.

8. Later, some fairly valuable paintings were displayed.

9. That boy is rather talented; he'll go far if he works hard.

10. The plumbers finally finished repairing the pipes today.

11. The archaeologist washed the artifact carefully.

12. Quite suddenly, the horse bolted across the field.

Adverbs in Comparisons

Use the comparative form of an adverb when you compare two actions. Use the superlative form of an adverb when you compare three or more actions.

For most adverbs that end in *-ly,* the comparative is formed with the word *more.* The superlative is formed with the word *most.*

quickly	more quickly	most quickly
carefully	more carefully	most carefully

For some adverbs, add *-er* for the comparative and *-est* for the superlative.

soon	sooner	soonest
fast	faster	fastest

Some adverbs change completely in the comparative and superlative.

well	better	best
much	more	most
little	less	least
far	farther	farthest

Using the Correct Forms of Adverbs Write the correct form of the adverb on the line.

1. Sue used the scissors (superlative of *carefully*). __________

2. John examined the evidence (comparative of *closely*) than I. __________

3. Which mason worked (superlative of *well*)? __________

4. The gears ran (comparative of *smoothly*). __________

5. I slept (comparative of *comfortably*) yesterday. __________

6. My friends went home (comparative of *early*). __________

7. Miko stuck to her task (superlative of *stubbornly*). __________

8. Ralph stopped (comparative of *soon*) than the others. __________

9. The ambassador traveled (superlative of *far*). __________

10. The batter hit the ball (comparative of *hard*) than I did. __________

11. Tortoises move (comparative of *slowly*) than hares. __________

12. Who can hold this note (superlative of *long*)? __________

Adjective or Adverb?

To decide whether to use an adjective or an adverb, examine the kind of word you want to modify.

An **adjective** modifies a noun or pronoun. An **adverb** modifies a verb, an adjective, or another adverb.

The children feel *bad* about their behavior. (*Bad* is a predicate adjective modifying *children.*)

The children behaved *badly.* (*Badly* is an adverb modifying the action verb *behaved.* It tells *how* the children behaved.)

Note: The word *good* is used as an adjective. The word *well* is used as an adverb, except when it refers to a person's health.

Choosing the Right Modifier Underline the correct word in parentheses.

1. Denise writes (good, well) enough to be published.
2. If you want people to read your report, type it (neat, neatly).
3. At the Japanese restaurant, the shrimp tempura tastes (good, well).
4. Priscilla looks quite (radiant, radiantly) in her wedding dress.
5. Rosa played the part of Lady Macbeth (real, really) well.
6. The driver who caused the accident feels very (bad, badly) about it.
7. Three deer walked (slow, slowly) across the meadow.
8. The trumpet solo in that song really sounds (nice, nicely).
9. The star that shines (brightest, most brightly) in the night sky is Sirius.
10. Marcia's black bean soup smells (wonderful, wonderfully).
11. Nick looked (furious, furiously) at the dented fender.
12. Diana drove the tractor (careful, carefully) up the ramp.
13. Those gardenias smell (fragrant, fragrantly).
14. These precious stones shine (beautiful, beautifully) in the light.
15. They look (beautiful, beautifully) now that they are polished.
16. After a week the milk turned (bad, badly) in the refrigerator.
17. By now it must smell pretty (bad, badly).
18. If Jason rides his bike that (bad, badly), he may hurt himself.
19. We talked (quieter, more quietly), since the baby was asleep.
20. Dolores did quite (good, well) on her final exams.

Linking Grammar and Writing: Using Adverbs

Answer each question with at least four adverbs. Then write a letter in which you describe your experience with a swarm of mosquitoes at a picnic. Use at least six of the listed adverbs. Follow good letter form.

1. How might a mosquito buzz? ______________________________
2. How might a mosquito bite? ______________________________
3. How might you shout? ______________________________
4. How might you swat a mosquito? ______________________________
5. How might you spray repellent? ______________________________

Additional Practice: Using Adverbs

Choosing the Right Modifier Underline the correct word in parentheses.

1. Does your brother play tennis (good, well) enough to compete?
2. Surprisingly, that odd outfit looks really (good, well) on you.
3. The rescue team had to move (slow, slowly) because of avalanche danger.
4. This time the emergency crew responded (quicker, more quickly).
5. I've heard that Chinese is a (real, really) difficult language to learn.
6. After a good tuneup, the engine ran (quiet, quietly).
7. Cut the paper (neat, neatly) and precisely to make that pattern.
8. The room looks (strange, strangely) through these tinted glasses.

Using Adverbs Correctly All of these sentences contain errors in the use of adverbs. Rewrite each sentence correctly.

1. The Concorde flies more faster than other airliners.

____

2. Of all the rings I've tried on, this one fits tightest.

____

3. I haven't never been able to repair anything like a watch.

____

4. That striped polo shirt is the least expensive of the two.

____

5. Teddy Roosevelt said to speak soft and carry a big stick.

____

6. Give directions good if you want us to find your place.

____

7. Danielle ran quicker than any of the other runners.

____

8. No copying machine operates more easier than this one.

____

Review: Using Adverbs

Finding the Adverbs Underline each adverb. Draw an arrow from the adverb to the word it modifies. Watch for double adverbs.

1. The careless skier limped very slowly with his new crutches.
2. The rolls baked by the class yesterday were quite good.
3. She copied the exercise extremely carefully.
4. I travel this road often, but it always has surprises.
5. Albert ate his lunch too fast, and now he feels somewhat ill.

Choosing the Right Modifier Underline the correct word in parentheses.

1. Renaldo smiled (bright, brightly) at the audience.
2. You ran around the track (quicker, more quickly) that time.
3. We all felt (good, well) about the outcome of the game.
4. The dog seemed (uneasy, uneasily) about something.
5. Melanie and Ron arrived (more early, earlier) than we expected.

Adding a Suitable Modifier Write suitable modifiers on the lines below.

1. The ________________ horse jumped ________________.
2. These snakes are ________________ ________________.
3. The ________________ boy entered the classroom ________________.
4. A ________________ woman appeared ________________ in the castle window.
5. My ________________ book fell ________________ to the floor.
6. ________________ I felt that life was grim, but today things look ________________.
7. The ________________ chef stormed ________________ out of the kitchen.
8. Donna tried ________________ to piece together her ________________ notes.

Skills Assessment 2

Handbooks 40–42

Directions One or more of the underlined sections in the following sentences may contain an error in grammar, usage, punctuation, spelling, or capitalization. Write the letter of each incorrect section. Then rewrite the section correctly. If there is no error in an item, write *E.*

Example The baseball coach rubbed his cheeks. The batter know
A B C
that this signal meant to swing at the next pitch. No error
D E

Answer C—knew

1. Will Rogers twirled his lasso real slowly. Then he drawled, “We are all
A B C
ignorant, but on different subjects.” No error
D E

2. The earths crust broke. Molten rock burst through and begun to form
A B C D
a volcanic mountain under the sea. No error
E

3. Each of the astronauts has a radio inside their spacesuit. There
A B
isn’t no air in space to carry the sound waves of human voices. No error
C D E

4. Some artists believe that Mary Cassatt painted as good as the great
A B C
french painters Degas and Manet, who were her friends. No error
D E

5. Laser beams are brighter and more narrower than ordinary beams of
A B
light. Never stare directly into a laser beam, it can hurt your eyes.
C D
No error
E

6. In 1947, Chuck Yeager flown an airplane more faster than the speed
A B C D
of sound. No error
E

7. After the early 1900s, jazz spread gradually from New Orleans to other
A B
areas of the United States. No error
C D E

8. In health class Mr. Cruz learned (A) us better (B) eating habits. He showed us (C) a list of foods with the greatest (D) amounts of nutrients for energy and growth. No error (E)

9. The artist carefully (A) lay (B) each tile. On (C) the floor of the art gallery. She created a colorful (D) mosaic. No error (E)

10. Mr. Watanabe really feels badly (A) that he didn't (B) have any (C) more of those (D) kites to sell you. No error (E)

11. Jane Addams founded Hull House in chicago. (A) Years ago, poor people come (B) there (C) and received (D) help. No error (E)

12. Maria Tallchief (A) rose (B) to fame as a great (C) star of the American (D) ballet. No error (E)

13. The mural *Ghosts of the Barrio* honors (A) some of the most famous (B) Mexican Americans. (C) Murals of these (D) kind are very common in East Los Angeles. No error (E)

14. Thomas Jefferson's (A) pet bird used to set (B) on his shoulder, but (C) he had to leave (D) the bird at Monticello. No error (E)

15. Maria Callas was one of the world's best (A) opera sopranoes. (B) Her voice sounded harsh (C) or sweetly, (D) depending on the role she was playing. No error (E)

Prepositions

A **preposition** is a word that relates its object to some other word in the sentence. The **object of a preposition** is the noun or pronoun following the preposition.

I strolled *along* the street. (*Along* is the preposition; *street* is its object. *Along* relates *street* to *strolled*.)

Here are some words often used as prepositions:

about	around	between	for	off	toward
above	as	beyond	from	on	under
across	before	but (except)	in	out	underneath
after	behind	by	inside	outside	until
against	below	down	into	over	up
along	beneath	during	near	past	with
among	beside	except	of	through	within
				to	without

Finding the Prepositions Underline the prepositions in the sentences.

1. Above her head sat the Cheshire cat.
2. The train roared through the tunnel, blasting its horn.
3. Everything in our lives had been fine before the tornado.
4. Sam brought his camera to the scene of the fire.
5. The fawn ran silently among the trees and disappeared from sight.
6. Several members of the group were late on the day of the vote.

Finding Prepositions and Their Objects In each sentence, underline each preposition. Then circle the object of each preposition.

Example Put the book on the (desk.)

1. Carol filled the grill with charcoal for the cookout.
2. On Tuesday my father's car was parked inside the garage.
3. Hundreds of people swarmed into the theater for the concert.
4. For a week the schooner was moored in the harbor.
5. Jan showed the lizard to her teacher before class.
6. At noon the colonel strode across the courtyard toward the gate.
7. Without doubt, spitting in the subway is against the law.
8. Our class has been running behind schedule until now.
9. Some of the disagreements between us are beside the point.
10. In the evenings of August the katydids sang in the trees.

Preposition or Adverb?

A number of words that are used as prepositions are also used as adverbs.

We fell *down.* (adverb)
We fell *down* the stairs. (preposition)

Such words, when they are used as adverbs, do not have objects. When they are used as prepositions, they do have objects.

Identifying Prepositions and Adverbs Decide whether the italicized word in each sentence is used as a preposition or an adverb. On the line provided, write *P* for *preposition* or *A* for *adverb.*

_______ **1.** *Over* our heads, great formations of geese were flying north.

_______ **2.** As they flew *over,* we thought we could hear their wild cries.

_______ **3.** Please ask the children to come *inside* because of the storm.

_______ **4.** With all that lightning, they will be safer *inside* the house.

_______ **5.** A new family has moved into that old house *down* the road from us.

_______ **6.** An ambulance stood *near* in case of an emergency.

_______ **7.** Tulips are growing all *along* the streets of Holland, Michigan.

_______ **8.** They reached the frontier; what lay *beyond* was unknown.

_______ **9.** After many years on the bench, the judge decided to step *down.*

_______ **10.** We went *outside* for a while because of the noise and smoke.

_______ **11.** When they were only halfway *up,* they were neither up nor down.

_______ **12.** Out *beyond* the solar system lies the vastness of space.

_______ **13.** No one *outside* their family knows the location of the gold.

_______ **14.** The cat fled *up* a tree while the dogs barked angrily below.

_______ **15.** *Near* the foot of that great old live oak tree is an ancient grave.

_______ **16.** If you go to the ballgame, why not ask your sister to go *along?*

Prepositional Phrases

A **prepositional phrase** is a group of words that begins with a preposition and ends with its object. Words that modify the object are also part of the phrase.

Brad found the pencils *in the big oak desk.*

When a preposition has more than one object, the construction is called a **compound object**. All the objects are part of the prepositional phrase.

I sat *beside Gary and his father.* (*Beside Gary and his father* is a prepositional phrase with a compound object.)

Finding the Prepositional Phrases Underline the prepositional phrases in the following sentences.

Example To his favorite aunt he gave a beautiful bouquet of flowers.

1. You can't park on this street during rush hour.
2. We haven't heard from Jack in almost two years.
3. During those long summer afternoons, we read books about pirates.
4. Then we sang by the light of the silvery moon.
5. I found an old photograph of my great-grandmother in the attic.
6. The Appian Way, built by the ancient Romans in the fourth century B.C., was part of their main route to Greece and the East.
7. *For Whom the Bell Tolls* is the title of a novel by Ernest Hemingway.
8. Planes roared over the trees and the houses and into the night.
9. After a while he turned around and trudged sadly toward town.
10. Maggie arrived on the dock with her father and her sister.
11. Grandma Moses, who painted scenes of American farm life, illustrated "'Twas the Night Before Christmas" at the age of one hundred.
12. Just between you and me, I know little about any flowers except roses.
13. Rabbits live in burrows and under piles of brush.
14. By now, air-cushion vehicles, or hovercraft, have been used for transportation in a number of places.
15. They say that peacocks often roost in trees at night.
16. Jim Gary makes sculptures of dinosaurs from old car parts.
17. Above all, don't try to cut that wood against the grain.
18. No one but a fool would run across the highway in that traffic.
19. Did you walk past the cemetery on Halloween?
20. That field of corn across the road from us will be gone within a year.

Pronouns as Objects of Prepositions

When a pronoun is used as the object of a preposition, its **object** form must be used. The object forms of pronouns are *me, us, you, her, him, it, them,* and *whom.*

Ann talked to *us.* We thought of *him.* Come with *me.*

Whom is the object form of the interrogative pronoun. *Who* is the subject form.

Who has the key? (*Who* is the subject.)
To *whom* did you give the key? (*Whom* is the object of *to.*)

Sometimes the object of a preposition is compound.

Take it to *John and him.*

To be sure you use the correct pronoun in a compound object, say the pronoun alone with its preposition. Then say it in the complete sentence.

Take it to (he, *him*). Take it to John and *him.*

Use *between* when the object of the preposition refers to two people or things. Use *among* when speaking of three or more.

Ginny sat between Nick and me. (two people)
Divide the profits among them all. (more than two)

Using Pronouns as Objects of Prepositions Underline the correct word in parentheses.

1. The magician stared directly at Paul and (I, me).
2. Between the edge of the woods and (we, us), there stretched a wide meadow.
3. I received an invitation from (she, her) and her parents.
4. We divided the responsibilities (between, among) the various members.
5. The answer to the problem was up to (they, them) and their friends.
6. For (who, whom) is that letter intended?
7. "There's nobody here but (we, us) chickens."
8. The orders had been given by the general and (he, him).
9. Stand directly behind (she, her) and (I, me).
10. A conflict developed (between, among) the two branches of government.
11. I asked her from (who, whom) she had received that beautiful ring.
12. There had been an agreement between (he, him) and (she, her).

Using Prepositional Phrases

A prepositional phrase, like an adjective or an adverb, modifies a word in the sentence.

Prepositional phrases do the same kind of work in sentences that adjectives and adverbs do. A prepositional phrase that modifies a noun or pronoun is an **adjective phrase.**

The cover *of the book* is blue.

A prepositional phrase that modifies a verb is an **adverb phrase.**

The football team practiced *after school.*

Identifying Prepositional Phrases Underline the prepositional phrase in each sentence, and circle the word it modifies. On the line write *ADJ* or *ADV* to indicate whether it is an adjective phrase or an adverb phrase.

Example ___ADJ___ The (girl) in the blue dress sat down.

________ **1.** Three campers decided to walk over the old wooden bridge.

________ **2.** After the game Angie drove us all home.

________ **3.** Four scientists from the space center watched the experiment.

________ **4.** Please put the magician's props behind the big box.

________ **5.** I saw a strange Siamese cat in the alley.

________ **6.** Acres of corn had been ruined.

________ **7.** The journey into the past was very exciting.

________ **8.** I would like to visit interesting lands beyond the sea.

________ **9.** The smoke drifted up the chimney.

________ **10.** The ground underneath the trees is still dry.

________ **11.** The explorers at the site made an important discovery.

________ **12.** That man in the striped shirt is the referee.

________ **13.** Juan found a dusty old strongbox in the basement.

________ **14.** We waited impatiently until the intermission.

________ **15.** Before him lay the great Pacific Ocean.

Beginning Sentences with Prepositional Phrases

For the sake of emphasis or variety, you may sometimes begin a sentence with a prepositional phrase.

We arrived at the station *in the morning.*
In the morning we arrived at the station.

It is not necessarily better to start a sentence with a prepositional phrase. However, a variety of sentence beginnings makes for more interesting reading.

Placing Prepositional Phrases Effectively Rewrite the following sentences so that each begins with a prepositional phrase. If the phrase is a long one, place a comma after it.

1. Several people waited nervously outside the hot, stuffy room.

___

___

2. The squirrel cautiously peeked out of its hole after the storm.

___

___

3. Father made a surprising announcement in the middle of dinner.

___

___

4. Steve walked home slowly after the exhausting game.

___

5. Tragedy struck out of the blue.

___

6. I'll go to visit my grandmother in the meantime.

___

7. The air was dry and crisp on that winter day.

___

8. Think carefully before you go ahead with your plan.

___

___

Placement of Prepositional Phrases

Sometimes a prepositional phrase can be moved from one position to another in a sentence without changing the meaning. At other times, however, the position of a prepositional phrase makes a great deal of difference in the meaning of a sentence.

Unclear The band played before the game in the end zone.
Clear The band played in the end zone before the game.

Placing Prepositional Phrases Correctly Rewrite the following sentences by changing the position of one prepositional phrase to make the meaning clearer.

1. Timothy mailed the letter to his grandmother in the post office.

____

____

2. A brown dog ran across the road with a long tail.

____

3. The clock stopped by the water fountain at 3:30.

____

4. Amanda threw her mother from the train a kiss.

____

5. In the cages we saw many exotic animals.

____

6. We took photographs of the sea on the pier.

____

7. Regina told us about the great vacation she had at lunch.

____

____

8. With long ears and an orange wig, the child laughed at the clown.

____

____

Conjunctions and Interjections

A **conjunction** is a word that connects words or groups of words.

Coordinating conjunctions join words or groups of words that are of equal importance. Some common coordinating conjunctions are *and, but,* and *or.*

Ken read *and* reviewed the chapter.
The letter was short *but* interesting.

An **interjection** is a word or short group of words used to express feeling. Interjections may be punctuated by exclamation points or commas.

Oh, no! I spilled the soup. *Yes,* I like soup.

Identifying Conjunctions and Interjections Underline the conjunctions and interjections in the following sentences. Write *C* above each conjunction and *I* above each interjection.

1. Lewis and Clark explored the West, and their story is fascinating.
2. Hooray! Vacation starts tomorrow.
3. No, I don't want to play soccer now.
4. The doctor quickly but carefully took charge, and order was restored.
5. Oh, my! It's been snowing all night, and our alley is blocked.
6. I've never met Ms. Phelps or Mr. Olson, but I've heard of them.
7. Well, the reporter listened and nodded but said nothing.
8. Yes! I said I'd clean my room, and I meant it!
9. We looked for a bus or a cab, but we ended up walking home.
10. Darn! My pen ran out of ink, and now my pencil's broken.
11. Well, I would like a sandwich and some milk.
12. The ship pitched and rolled on the stormy sea.
13. Wow! Do you call that good pitching or not?
14. Well, well, what have we here?
15. Sure, the music was modern, but it was romantic too.
16. Gosh, I hope Nancy will understand or at least listen.

Linking Grammar and Writing: Using Prepositions, Conjunctions, and Interjections

Choose two classmates. Ask them questions about their likes and dislikes—for example,

What is your favorite singing group?
What are two of your favorite Saturday activities?
What is the best program on television?
Who are the two people you admire the most?
Which of your classes do you like the most?
What is your least favorite chore?

Take notes on the answers. Then write five sentences comparing and contrasting the two classmates. Use a conjunction to connect the subjects in one sentence and a conjunction to join the objects in another. Begin a third sentence with a prepositional phrase, and end a fourth sentence with one. Finally, write at least one sentence containing an interjection.

1. ____________________

____

____

2. ____________________

____

____

3. ____________________

____

____

4. ____________________

____

____

5. ____________________

____

____

Additional Practice: Using Prepositions, Conjunctions, and Interjections

Finding Prepositions and Adverbs Three of the sentences below contain prepositions. The rest contain adverbs. Underline the preposition or adverb in each sentence and write *Preposition* or *Adverb* on the line. If the word is a preposition, circle its object. Also circle all interjections.

1. Yes, Leo brought his cousin along. ______________

2. Near the house towered a huge oak. ______________

3. Hey! That bus passed us by. ______________

4. A hot-air balloon floated over the treetops. ______________

5. The crowd was silent during the performance. ______________

6. True, a few people did get left behind. ______________

7. Yuck! Nobody took the garbage out. ______________

8. I collected the geranium pots and brought them inside. ______________

Using Adjective and Adverb Phrases Rewrite each sentence, adding the prepositional phrase shown in parentheses. Be sure to place the phrase correctly. On the short line, write whether you used the phrase as an adjective (*ADJ*) or an adverb (*ADV*). Then underline the word the phrase modifies.

1. The building is the state capitol. (on the hill)

____ __________

____ __________

2. The pattern interested us. (on the turtle's shell)

____ __________

____ __________

3. Carol stared at the sculpture. (with a puzzled expression)

____ __________

____ __________

4. Ramon stared at the sculpture. (on the brass pedestal)

____ __________

____ __________

Review: Using Prepositions, Conjunctions, and Interjections

Finding the Prepositional Phrases Underline the prepositional phrase in each of the following sentences. Circle the object (or objects) of the preposition. On the line, write *Adjective* if the phrase is an adjective phrase. Write *Adverb* if the phrase is an adverb phrase.

Example The girl with the braces smiled. *Adjective*

1. A bloodhound sniffed around the garage. ______
2. Everybody inside the cabin was a skier. ______
3. Mr. Jones was a witness for the prosecution. ______
4. The left side of the bleachers needs repair. ______
5. Mary usually sits with Ellen and her. ______

Identifying Prepositions and Adverbs Identify each word in italics by writing *Preposition* or *Adverb.*

1. The ship went *down* fast. ______
2. *Under* no circumstances should you leave. ______
3. We looked *inside,* but the room was empty. ______
4. The firefighter climbed *out* the window. ______
5. May we come *along* too? ______
6. We waited forever for the ship to pass *through.* ______

Using Conjunctions and Interjections Circle the conjunctions and underline the interjections in the following sentences.

1. Wow! Did you see how hard and far he hit that ball?
2. Yes, Anne or Marlene will be president of the class.
3. Sure, the movie was long, but it was exciting.
4. Weston read a book about stamps and coins.
5. Well, was the message for him or for me?

What Are Compound Sentences?

A **simple sentence** is a sentence with only one subject and one predicate. Both the subject and the predicate of a simple sentence may be compound.

A **compound sentence** consists of two or more simple sentences joined together. The parts of a compound sentence are joined either by a comma and a coordinating conjunction (*and, but, or*) or by a semicolon (;).

> We earned nine dollars, *and* we put it in the bank.
> The sun was up; the morning beckoned.

Using compound sentences helps to make your writing more interesting and readable.

Analyzing Compound Sentences Underline the subject once and the verb twice in each part of the compound sentence. Circle the conjunction or semicolon.

Example I saw the light, (and) I followed it.

1. Toshi went to the mall on Saturday, but Jody stayed home.
2. Ms. Ballak may be in court, or she may be in her office.
3. Snow fell; winter was now upon us.
4. I wrote her several times, but I never got an answer.
5. We could play a video game, or we could go to Jim's house.
6. Lawyers argue cases, but judges decide them.
7. Greg shoveled the snow, and his brother began a snow sculpture.
8. Charlene clutched at the brake, and the bike finally stopped.
9. Everyone played pretty well, but Jenny scored the winning basket.
10. You can walk to school today, or you can take the bus.
11. She calls it a dragonfly; I call it a darning needle.
12. The clown made a face; the child burst into laughter.
13. Kathy phoned this morning, but our phone was out of order.
14. The boat nosed up to the dock; our trip was finally over.
15. He plays sports a great deal, but he studies hard too.
16. Lou has been baking bread; Connie is making a big salad.

Compound Sentence or Compound Verb?

You will often need to know the difference between a compound sentence and a simple sentence with a compound verb.

> Tony *washed* and *dried* the dishes.
> (This is a simple sentence. The conjunction *and* joins two parts of a compound verb.)
>
> *Tony washed the dishes,* and *I dried them.*
> (This is a compound sentence. The conjunction *and* joins two simple sentences, each with its own subject and verb.)

Identifying Compound Predicates and Compound Sentences
Decide whether each sentence is a compound sentence or a simple sentence with a compound verb. Write either *CS* (compound sentence) or *CV* (compound verb) on the line provided. Underline any compound subjects.

CV **1.** The motorcycles roared around the curve and raced down the track.

CS **2.** Gina and Dave picked the wildflowers, and we arranged them.

CS **3.** Her mother went to the trade show, but Doreen stayed home.

CV **4.** Did you and Lee walk or ride to your dance class?

CS **5.** Several people listened, but nobody volunteered.

CV **6.** Jaime and Ana sorted the photos and then framed them.

CS **7.** Jaime did most of the work; Ana helped.

_____ **8.** The subway car slowed down and finally stopped.

_____ **9.** Will you stay home, or will you come with us to the movies?

_____ **10.** The whale shark is the largest of all fish, but it does not attack people.

_____ **11.** Margarita hurt her leg, but she didn't complain.

_____ **12.** Tom and Gail quickly cut and stacked the firewood.

_____ **13.** Gail cut the wood, and Tom stacked it.

_____ **14.** Rain or snow may fall, but I won't change my plan.

_____ **15.** The squirrel found and buried the nut.

_____ **16.** Wang and his brother looked at the problem and spotted the solution.

Writing and Punctuating Compound Sentences

When the parts of a compound sentence are joined by a coordinating conjunction, a *comma* precedes the conjunction. Otherwise, the parts are separated by a *semicolon.*

Use commas in compound sentences to clarify meaning. In very short compound sentences, however, you will not need to use commas. The meaning will be clear.

Jerry rode to school, and Karen and Ed walked. (comma used for clarity)
Jerry rode to school; Karen and Ed walked. (semicolon used for clarity)
Jerry rode and we walked. (meaning of sentence is clear)

Punctuating Compound Constructions Where needed, add commas or semicolons to the following sentences. If the sentence is correct, write *C* before it.

_______ **1.** The hare slept and the tortoise ran.

_______ **2.** Our school play is tonight and we are a bit nervous.

_______ **3.** The auction started the first bidder bought three goblets.

_______ **4.** Susan might study law or she might study medicine.

_______ **5.** Carlos bought a tie but he still needed a jacket.

_______ **6.** Andrea likes to play soccer her brother prefers swimming.

_______ **7.** Dave played an accompaniment and Karen danced.

_______ **8.** The polar bear suddenly stopped and then it turned and faced the hunter.

_______ **9.** Amy can play the guitar or she can play the piano.

_______ **10.** George speaks German but he also speaks French.

_______ **11.** We walked in and they walked out.

_______ **12.** The siren went off suddenly I jumped.

_______ **13.** Luke and Mark played checkers and Mark won.

_______ **14.** I like peanuts but I also like cashews.

_______ **15.** José and Nick studied for the test and they both did well.

_______ **16.** Dee read her essay aloud but Marcy chose to hand in a written report.

Writing Good Compound Sentences

You have learned that a compound sentence consists of two or more simple sentences joined together. However, the parts of a compound sentence must express thoughts that are related to each other.

Unrelated Patricia rode her bike. My bike has a flat tire.
Related Patricia rode her bike, *but* I had to walk.

Some pairs of sentences make good compound sentences, and some do not. The pairs must be related in thought.

Making Compound Sentences Find the six sentence pairs that could be compound sentences. Rewrite them, using a comma and a coordinating conjunction. For pairs that should not be combined, write *No compound.*

N **1.** Renée enjoyed seeing her old friends. She wore her new jeans.

____

Y **2.** We could go bowling. We could go to a movie.

____

Y **3.** The President will sign the bill. He might wait a week.

____

4. Jumbo jets are built for comfort. I once flew on a 747.

____

5. Keith completed the test. He forgot to write his name on it.

____

____

6. Leaves fell from the trees. The oak is over one hundred years old.

____

7. The cars were wrecked. The passengers were unharmed.

____

____

8. You can take the bus downtown. You can take the subway.

____

____

What Are Complex Sentences?

A **complex sentence** is a sentence that contains one main clause and one or more subordinate clauses.

A **clause** is a group of words that contains a subject and a verb. There are two types of clauses: main clauses and subordinate clauses.

A **main clause,** also called an independent clause, can stand alone as a sentence. A simple sentence has one main clause. A compound sentence has two or more main clauses.

The weather changed; we went outside.

A **subordinate clause** also has a subject and a predicate, but it cannot stand by itself as a sentence. It is often introduced by a **subordinating conjunction,** such as *when, if, because,* or *until.*

Because the weather changed   when we went outside

Analyzing Complex Sentences In each of the following complex sentences, find the subordinate clause. Underline its subject once and its verb twice. Then circle the subordinating conjunction.

Example Although our team fought hard, we finally lost the game.

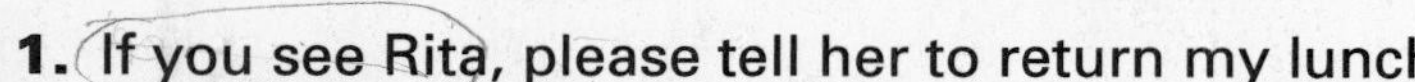

1. If you see Rita, please tell her to return my lunch box.
2. When my grandmother was young, she listened to Frank Sinatra records.
3. Until you change those strings, your banjo won't sound very good.
4. Please look after my dog until I come home.
5. Unless I am wrong, peaches were first grown in China.
6. Bring your backpack when you come to school today.
7. Since Eldon hates airplanes, he'll probably take the train.
8. While supplies last, let's get Dad one of these T-shirts.
9. Write about your experience while it is fresh in your mind.
10. Although we are ready, the ground is still too wet to plow.
11. Where there is smoke, there may be fire.
12. "Don't fire until you see the whites of their eyes."
13. I'll give you that book after I have finished it.
14. Someone forgot to water the roses, as you can see.
15. Wherever you go, you'll find interesting people.
16. Look before you leap.

Identifying Sentence Structure

Analyzing Sentences In the following sentences, underline each main clause once and each subordinate clause twice.

1. Just thinking is not enough; you must think of something.
2. The last car of this poky old freight train is just now coming into view, way down the line.
3. You should clean your lens so that your photos will be clear.
4. Don't ride on a motorcycle unless you have a helmet.
5. I'll go if I can.
6. Spring came and went pretty quickly.
7. I'll wash; you dry.
8. Leave when you have finished.
9. We tried but we failed.
10. When people can choose any action, they usually imitate one another.
11. Do you remember the name of Robert Burton's book?
12. Although my dog can play the piano, he does not play it well.
13. Can you imagine the enormous size of the Milky Way galaxy?
14. We had gone only a little way into the cave before our flashlight went out.
15. After forty days Noah sent forth a dove, but the dove returned.
16. Plenty of people despise money, but few know how to give it away.
17. No bird soars too high if he soars with his own wings.
18. Is the universe expanding, or is it contracting?
19. If you've never tried it, don't knock it.
20. The Great Barrier Reef forms a natural breakwater for the coast of northeast Australia and attracts tourists from all over the world.
21. Stay a little longer if you like.
22. How much music can they put on one compact disc?
23. In this plan you pay as you go.
24. Take it or leave it.
25. After the last song, the musicians packed up their instruments and got back on the bus.

Linking Grammar and Writing: Using Compound and Complex Sentences

Inside every fortune cookie is a slip of paper with a message. The message predicts the future or comments on an idea such as success, fame, or happiness. Here is an example:

You will earn | *great sums of money,* | *but you will* | *spend foolishly.*

Make up four messages that might be found in fortune cookies. Each message should be a compound sentence. Use more than one type of coordinating conjunction in your messages.

1. ______________________________

____

2. ______________________________

____

3. ______________________________

____

4. ______________________________

____

Imagine that you are a radio sportscaster describing a professional sports event or game. Write four sentences of dialogue that you might say in your broadcast. Use all three sentence types: simple, compound, and complex.

1. ______________________________

____

2. ______________________________

____

3. ______________________________

____

4. ______________________________

____

Additional Practice: Using Compound and Complex Sentences

Identifying Main and Subordinate Clauses In the following sentences, underline each main clause once and each subordinate clause twice.

1. A meteoroid, a piece of rock flying through space, approaches our planet at something like forty miles per second.
2. It hits the earth's atmosphere and gets hot; then it usually burns up.
3. People on the ground see a meteor—a "shooting star."
4. When a meteor lands on the earth, it is called a meteorite.
5. It may be small, or it may cause great damage and dig a huge crater.
6. Some scientists see chemical evidence of life on these space objects.
7. If you have a sailboat with two parallel hulls, you've got a catamaran.
8. It's fast but it's stable.

Making Compound Sentences Find the three sentence pairs that can be combined into compound sentences. Rewrite them, using a suitable coordinating conjunction and correct punctuation. For pairs that should not be combined, write *No compound.*

1. My brother loves horror movies. I usually prefer comedies myself.

   ____

   ____

2. Frost destroyed some of the crops. One popular vegetable is corn.

   ____

   ____

3. Lightning crackled in the sky. Rain began to fall.

   ____

   ____

4. We took a train to Denver. Locomotives used to be powered by steam.

   ____

   ____

Review: Using Compound and Complex Sentences

Combining Sentences Combine each pair of sentences. Follow the directions in parentheses. In a simple sentence, use a compound subject or a compound verb. In compound and complex sentences, use the indicated conjunctions. Don't forget to use commas where necessary.

1. Many are called. Few are chosen. (Compound, *but*)

____

2. I had fallen asleep. I did not hear the doorbell ring. (Simple)

____

3. The skydivers opened their parachutes. They floated to the ground. (Compound, *and*)

____

____

4. He planted apple seeds. He went. (Complex, *wherever*)

____

5. Building kites can be fun. Flying kites can be fun. (Simple)

____

6. I haven't seen my cousin. She visited us last summer. (Complex, *since*)

____

____

7. Elspeth went into town. She got her skates sharpened. (Simple)

____

8. Eat those apples. They'll just spoil. (Compound, *or*)

____

9. Writing good sentences takes practice. We all know. (Complex, *as*)

____

10. We might go to the movies tonight. We might stay home. (Compound, *or*)

____

____

Agreement of Subject and Verb

A verb must agree with its subject in **number**. The number of a word refers to whether it is singular (one thing or action) or plural (more than one thing or action).

The *donkeys* (plural) *were* (plural) braying.
He (singular) *has* (singular) a bass guitar.

Here are some important things to remember:

1. Often a phrase appears between the subject and the verb. The simple subject is never part of that phrase. Do not mistake the phrase or any word in it for the subject.

   Each of the houses *was* brown. Four *barrels* of oil *were* shipped.

2. The pronoun *you* is never used with a singular verb. It is always used with plural verbs.

   You *were* very helpful. You *understand* my problem.

3. The pronoun *I* is most often used with a plural verb. The only singular verb forms used with *I* are *am* and *was.*

   I *am* an artist. I *run* every morning.
   I *was* a student. I *like* the sound of bongo drums.

Making Subject and Verb Agree Underline the correct form of the verb in each of the following sentences.

1. The glass in the mirror (is, are) badly scratched.

2. Several people in the audience (was, were) coughing.

3. I (doesn't, don't) want to hurt anybody's feelings.

4. Special moments at a family reunion (means, mean) a great deal.

5. One of these three shells (is, are) covering a pea.

6. The days of our summer vacation (flies, fly) by quickly.

7. You (was, were) the only one I missed at the party.

8. Which one of the hospitals (has, have) visiting hours for children?

9. The car with the broken windows (is, are) still in the street.

10. I'm sure you (is, are) the best player on the hockey team.

11. These books about magic (deals, deal) mostly with card tricks.

12. We think our policy in these matters (is, are) fair.

13. The profits from the sale (goes, go) into our scholarship fund.

14. The remarks by the President (was, were) misquoted.

15. I, as the oldest child, often (takes, take) care of my sisters.

Verbs with Compound Subjects

A **compound subject** consists of two or more subjects that share the same verb. When a compound subject contains the conjunction *and,* it is plural; therefore, a plural verb must be used with it.

Lettie and Brenda are friends. (The compound subject is *Lettie and Brenda.* The verb *are* is plural.)

When the parts of a compound subject are joined by *or* or *nor,* the verb agrees with the nearer subject.

Neither Bob nor his sisters *are* home.
The older boys or Tim *is* responsible for this work.

Using the Right Verb with a Compound Subject Underline the correct form of the verb in each of the following sentences.

1. Kerosene or other solvents (is, are) causing this pollution.
2. Mr. Brill and the other people (has, have) suggested a solution.
3. Neither Sally nor her brothers (is, are) able to be here.
4. The green shirt and the blue jacket (goes, go) together pretty well.
5. Warm, sunny days and cool nights (helps, help) grapes grow.
6. The freshness and the flavor (seems, seem) to be missing.
7. I think Kim or Lee (has, have) an extra notebook.
8. Our cows and our goat always (gets, get) enough to eat.
9. Several teenagers and an elderly man (was, were) waiting for the bus.
10. My Siamese cat and Juan's often (stares, stare) at each other.
11. Dennis and Denise (is, are) twins.
12. Neither rainstorms nor snowfall (stops, stop) our mail carrier.
13. Mozart and Haydn (was, were) both eighteenth-century composers.
14. Jill and her former schoolmates (meets, meet) once a month.
15. The chickens and the pig (belongs, belong) to my grandmother.
16. Clay necklaces or a papier-mâché mobile (is, are) going to be our class project.
17. Alligators and crocodiles (looks, look) somewhat similar.
18. My parents and my teacher (agrees, agree).
19. Neither a parachute nor an ejector seat (is, are) totally safe in an accident.
20. Caterpillars or a colorful butterfly always (fascinates, fascinate) me.
21. Neither the towels nor the shampoo (is, are) on the bathroom shelf.
22. San Juan and Mayagüez (was, were) the highlights of my trip to Puerto Rico.

Agreement in Inverted Sentences

In most sentences, the subject comes before the verb, as in "The long-lost *key was* in my pocket." For emphasis or variety, however, a writer or speaker might say, "In my pocket *was* the long-lost *key*." This sentence is called an **inverted sentence** because the subject of the sentence and its verb have changed positions. In inverted sentences, as in ordinary ones, the subject and the verb must agree. Word order does not affect subject-verb agreement.

Using the Right Verbs in Inverted Sentences Underline the correct form of the verb in each sentence.

1. Between Janice and me (sits, sit) the little cocker spaniel.
2. Waiting at the door (was, were) two meter readers.
3. Along the river banks (wanders, wander) a grizzled old prospector.
4. (Is, Are) high-rise buildings allowed along the lake shore?
5. Suddenly, out of the bushes (flies, fly) a mallard.
6. Into the distance (rides, ride) the Lone Ranger and his faithful companion, Tonto.
7. Underneath the brush (is, are) the pine cones.
8. Against the side of the house (leans, lean) the tired painter.
9. As the alarm sounds, down the pole (slides, slide) the firefighters.
10. On the banquet table (was, were) delicious strawberries.
11. Near the palace (marches, march) the soldiers.
12. Over our heads (thunders, thunder) an elevated train.
13. (Does, Do) the child and her parents have adequate shelter?
14. After the monkeys (comes, come) the elephant.
15. With our congratulations (goes, go) our sincere hope for your success.
16. Among the back pages (is, are) an index.
17. Over the stadium (floats, float) hundreds of balloons.
18. Outside the hall (stands, stand) several anxious reporters.
19. Above our heads (shines, shine) Vega, one of the brightest stars.
20. Around the large cage (flies, fly) the colorful parakeets.
21. After the last chapter (comes, come) a glossary and the bibliography.
22. In North Africa (lives, live) desert people called Bedouins.
23. Behind those buildings (is, are) my favorite Chinese restaurant.
24. Down the road (comes, come) three old circus wagons drawn by horses.
25. Red and orange (glows, glow) the campfire.

Verbs with There, Where, *and* Here

Often the word *there, where,* or *here* is used to begin a sentence. Its purpose is to get the sentence going. The subject appears later in the sentence. The subject and verb, however, must still agree.

There *is* a note on the desk.
(*Note* is the subject.)

Here *are* your gloves.
(*Gloves* is the subject.)

Where *are* my skates?
(*Skates* is the subject.)

Is there a gift for Bob?
(*Gift* is the subject.)

Using the Correct Verb Underline the correct form of the verb in each sentence.

1. Where (is, are) the student council meeting?
2. There (was, were) many gold miners in California in the 1800s.
3. Here (is, are) the songbook you asked for.
4. (Is, Are) there any other museums like this?
5. Where (is, are) the players from the baseball team?
6. There (is, are) too many people in this elevator.
7. (Is, Are) there a rooster or hens in the yard?
8. There (was, were) a severe thunderstorm last night.
9. Here (is, are) the speaker for the lecture.
10. Where (is, are) the parsnips that we brought in from the garden?
11. There (is, are) a large brown squirrel in that tree.
12. Where (was, were) the pandas hiding?
13. (Is, Are) there more cheese sandwiches in the kitchen?
14. (Is, Are) there some problem with your new VCR?
15. Here (is, are) your phone messages.
16. (Is, Are) there comments or a question for the speaker?
17. Where (was, were) the brown mitten when you found it?
18. Here (is, are) the last contestant in the spelling bee.
19. There (was, were) a basket of blueberries in the refrigerator.
20. Where (is, are) the clothes that need laundering?
21. Here (is, are) where the Battle of Lexington took place.
22. There (isn't, aren't) many neighbors as nice as Mr. Lofton.
23. (Is, Are) there one sock that doesn't have a hole in it?
24. Where (is, are) my hammer and wrench?

Agreement with Indefinite Pronouns

Singular verbs are used with singular indefinite pronouns. Plural verbs are used with plural indefinite pronouns.

Indefinite Pronouns

Singular			**Plural**
another	either	nobody	both
anybody	everybody	no one	few
anyone	everyone	one	many
anything	everything	somebody	several
each	neither	someone	

Singular Everyone here *is* a student.
Plural Few of us *are* wealthy.

The indefinite pronouns *all, any, most, none,* and *some* may be either singular or plural, depending on their meaning in sentences.

Singular Most of the room *is* clean.
Plural Most of the windows *are* washed.

Using the Right Verbs with Indefinite Pronouns Underline the correct form of the verb in each sentence.

1. Some of Death Valley (lies, lie) below sea level.
2. In the 1800s one of the valley's attractions (was, were) its deposits of borax.
3. Few of the world's deserts (has, have) higher temperatures than Death Valley.
4. Many of the plants in that region (has, have) ways of conserving water.
5. Another of California's interesting places (is, are) Joshua Tree National Monument.
6. Neither of these places (is, are) close to where I live.
7. One of the natural wonders of the world (is, are) the Grand Canyon.
8. No one (was, were) more impressed by that astounding sight than I.
9. Several of the students in my class (has, have) gone to see it.
10. Everybody (is, are) amazed when viewing the canyon for the first time.
11. Many of the visitors (descends, descend) to the Colorado River below.
12. Some (departs, depart) from the southern rim, some from the northern.
13. Either of the starting points (is, are) suitable.
14. Each of my memories of the Grand Canyon (is, are) pleasant.
15. None of the time I spent on those trips (was, were) wasted.
16. Another of the activities in the canyon (is, are) raft trips down the Colorado.

Linking Grammar and Writing: Understanding Subject and Verb Agreement

Select a recent television program. Then complete the following sentences. Either criticize or praise the program.

1. The star ______________________________

2. The first and second halves of the program ______________________________

____

3. I ______________________________

4. The actors in the show ______________________________

In the space below, write a letter to the television station that broadcast the program you selected, expressing your opinion about it. Use three of the five sentences above in your letter.

____

____

____

____

____

____

______________________________ :

____

____

____

____

____

____

____

Additional Practice: Understanding Subject and Verb Agreement

Choosing the Correct Verb Underline the correct verb.

1. Marty and her cousin (works, work) at the amusement park.
2. There (is, are) paper plates in the pantry.
3. In the lobby of the bank (stands, stand) a guard.
4. Where (was, were) the spelling errors in my paper?
5. Neither the hat nor the gloves (was, were) in the closet.
6. (Is, Are) the band or the cheerleaders out on the field now?
7. Everyone (has, have) been asking about that new teacher.
8. Beneath the city streets (runs, run) a busy subway line.
9. Either carrot sticks or an apple (makes, make) a nutritious snack.
10. Around the edges of the yard (grows, grow) lilac bushes.
11. The glass figurines on the shelf (is, are) fragile.
12. You (is, are) going to be designing the set.
13. Under the bridges (flows, flow) the Missouri River.
14. There (was, were) several reasons for the parade's delay.
15. Only one of these knives (has, have) been sharpened.
16. Here (is, are) the best-qualified person for the coaching position.
17. Everything in those downtown stores (looks, look) expensive.
18. Behind the shed (is, are) several stacks of wooden crates.
19. There (is, are) another strand of yellow lights in the box.
20. The lights on that strand (was, were) replaced last year.
21. Esther or Erin (is, are) suitable for that job.
22. There (is, are) apples and boxes of raisins to give out on Halloween.
23. Across the river (glimmers, glimmer) the headlights of predawn commuters.
24. (Is, Are) you the one who plays the harmonica so well?
25. Into the shopping malls (pours, pour) the holiday crowd.
26. Where (does, do) those palominos graze during the winter?
27. Beyond the giant tortoise (was, were) two platypuses.
28. The staples in this stapler (is, are) always getting jammed.
29. Anyone in our schools (is, are) eligible to compete for the prize.
30. I (needs, need) help with this homework assignment.

Review: Understanding Subject and Verb Agreement

Making Subjects and Verbs Agree Underline the correct verb.

1. Stephanie and her father (plays, play) baseball.
2. Here (is, are) the musicians from the orchestra.
3. One of the giant sequoia trees (stands, stand) upon the hill.
4. Neither of our pitchers (is, are) well enough to play.
5. Three pears and one orange (does, do) not make a fruit salad.
6. That roller coaster in the amusement park (sounds, sound) awesome.
7. Only one of the planets (was, were) visible that night.
8. Thatched huts and concrete buildings (contrasts, contrast) greatly.
9. Each of the ailing canaries (has, have) gotten proper care.
10. I (has, have) given you my opinion.
11. Neither you nor Beth (appears, appear) nervous.
12. (Is, Are) there any good novels on these shelves?
13. In the movie, Tom and his friends (goes, go) to the beach.
14. Everything on these shelves (is, are) on sale today.
15. There (is, are) thirteen stripes on our flag.
16. Through a crack in the wall (peers, peer) a mouse.
17. Either Francine or Greta (is, are) the drummer.
18. You (is, are) the winner of the funny-face contest.
19. (Does, Do) every record have scratches?
20. Around the lantern (swarms, swarm) the mosquitoes.
21. (Wasn't, Weren't) there any other Valentine's Day decorations?
22. My older sisters or my dad usually (cooks, cook) dinner.
23. Either the dentist or his assistants (prepares, prepare) the patient.
24. Through the treetops (shines, shine) the moon.
25. Either Anna or the twins (has, have) my record album.
26. Neither the mountains nor the seashore (offers, offer) Ben the setting he seeks.
27. Here (is, are) the answers to the math problems you worked on.
28. Into the night (creeps, creep) the cunning raccoons.
29. There (goes, go) the new instructor Li praised so highly.
30. Asparagus and broccoli (makes, make) a perfect addition to this pasta dish.

Skills Assessment 3

Directions One or more of the underlined sections in the following sentences may contain an error in grammar, usage, punctuation, spelling, or capitalization. Write the letter of each incorrect section. Then rewrite the section correctly. If there is no error in an item, write *E.*

Example The rings of the planet saturn is a spectacular
A B
sight, and you can see them through a telescope. No error
C D E
Answer A—Saturn; B—are

1. In 1832, around 40 percent of all factory workers in New England were
A
among the ages of seven and seventeen. Few of these children was
B C D
able to go to school. No error
E

2. Behind the huge painting on the wall is a secret safe. The butler or the
A B
maid know the combination. No error
C D E

3. Nellie Melba and Luisa Tetrazzini were famous singers who's names
A
were given to specially prepared dishes. Chefs invented peach melba
B C
and chicken tetrazzini in they're honor. No error
D E

4. Superman came from the planet Krypton, and grew up in the
A B C
Midwestern town of Smallville. Jonathan and Martha Kent was
D
his foster parents. No error
E

5. Some of these chinese kites is shaped like fish, and others look like
A B C D
dragons. No error
E

6. A diamond does not sparkle brilliantly in it's rough form, an uncut
A B C
diamond may look like a dull white stone. No error
D E

7. The segments of a rattlesnakes tail fits together loosely and make
A B C
a buzzing sound when shaken. No error
D E

8. One of the <u>greatest</u> **A** baseball players <u>were</u> **B** Babe Ruth. He <u>became</u> **C** a superstar in the <u>1920s and</u> **D** many fans flocked to ballparks to see him. <u>No error</u> **E**

9. <u>Wow. The</u> **A** hockey player <u>scored</u> **B** three goals in one game. This <u>amazeing</u> **C** feat <u>is</u> **D** called a hat trick. <u>No error</u> **E**

10. The tour guide at the art museum explained <u>those</u> **A** valuable paintings to Carla and <u>I.</u> **B** <u>There</u> **C** <u>kept</u> **D** in a special gallery. <u>No error</u> **E**

11. Although some people speak <u>English</u> **A** in <u>Morocco. The</u> **B** <u>country's</u> **C** three major languages <u>are</u> **D** Arabic, Berber, and French. <u>No error</u> **E**

12. There <u>are</u> **A** many incredible <u>stories</u> **B** about American folk <u>heroes.</u> **C** Pecos Bill, for example, <u>rode</u> **D** a cyclone across three states. <u>No error</u> **E**

13. Can <u>jewelry</u> **A** prevent <u>sickness or</u> **B** bring good luck? Some ancient people <u>beleived</u> **C** certain jewelry had <u>magical</u> **D** powers. <u>No error</u> **E**

14. Have you read <u>Laurence Yep's</u> **A** books *Child of the Owl* and *Sea Glass?* **B** Both of <u>these</u> **C** books <u>are</u> **D** about Chinese Americans. <u>No error</u> **E**

15. Where <u>are</u> **A** the <u>islands</u> **B** of St. Pierre and <u>Miquelon?</u> **C** To <u>who</u> **D** do they belong? <u>No error</u> **E**

Proper Nouns and Proper Adjectives (I)

Capitalize proper nouns and proper adjectives.

A **common noun** is the name of a whole class of persons, places, things, or ideas. A common noun is not capitalized.

girl   country   continent   language   patriotism

A **proper noun** is the name of a particular person, place, thing, or idea. A proper noun is always capitalized.

Sandra   **F**rance   **A**sia   **G**reen **B**ay **P**ackers   **S**tatue of **L**iberty

A **proper adjective** is an adjective formed from a proper noun.

French   **A**sian   **I**slamic   **E**lizabethan   **A**ppalachian

Using Capital Letters Correctly Write capital letters where they are needed above the words in the following sentences.

1. We are sailing soon to the windward islands.
2. The library of congress is searching for the document.
3. There is a rain forest on the malay peninsula.
4. The smallest of the fifty states is rhode island.
5. Do the people of australia live upside down?
6. I think james and julie have qualified for the boston marathon.
7. What is the british spelling of *color?*
8. The people of venice, italy, use boats to get around the city.
9. Where will the super bowl be played this year?
10. My friend marie plays the french horn in our local orchestra.
11. The romans used to like to watch chariot races.
12. They say the leaning tower of pisa leans a little more each year.
13. Did fred get any good pictures of the golden gate bridge?
14. I stood amazed in times square.
15. The united states supreme court will rule on that question shortly.
16. Recent rains have raised the level of the rio grande.
17. My sister will go to wheaton college in illinois.
18. The highest mountain in new zealand is mount cook.
19. Where did eve learn to speak portuguese so fluently?
20. A doctor named arthur conan doyle wrote the sherlock holmes stories.

Proper Nouns and Proper Adjectives (II)

Capitalize the **names and titles of persons,** and also the **initials or abbreviations** that stand for those names or titles.

Dr. **M**artin **L**uther **K**ing, **J**r. — **L**ieutenant **C**arol **S**mith
the lieutenant — **W**u **L**ee, **M.D.**

Capitalize **titles of persons and groups** whose rank is very important.

The **P**resident and **H**er **M**ajesty met at the White House.
The **V**ice-**P**resident introduced the **S**peaker of the **H**ouse.

Capitalize such words as ***mother, father, aunt,*** and ***uncle*** when these words are used as names.

Has **D**ad made dinner? — My father visited **A**unt **L**ouise at her office.

Capitalize the pronoun ***I.***

Did you see what **I** saw?

Capitalize all words referring to the **Deity,** to the **Holy Family,** and to **religious scriptures.**

God — **Y**ahweh — the **G**ospels — the **T**almud — the **K**oran

Using Capital Letters Correctly Write capital letters where they are needed above the words in the following sentences.

1. Our mayor flew to washington to speak to the vice-president.
2. Will mr. and mrs. fleming be here in time for dinner?
3. Do i have to see dr. sampson at his office?
4. Julius irving is called dr. j.
5. During the meeting, rabbi michael geller and father paul green, s.j., discussed community needs.
6. Georgia was named after king george II of England.
7. Last night david and i studied the talmud.
8. Is mother upstairs, or did she go to pick up dad?
9. The man in uniform is major alan burrows.
10. At 10:30, father o'keefe read from the bible.
11. Lady diana spencer became princess diana in 1981.
12. Mary and i saw boris becker play tennis.
13. Did you give aunt tess and uncle bill their presents?
14. The award was presented to mr. richard thomas and ms. irene samuels.
15. Although dad went with us, my mother did not.
16. Did you see the documentary about mother teresa?

Geographical Names

Capitalize major words in **geographical names.**

Continents North America, Asia
Bodies of Water the Indian Ocean, the Baltic Sea, Hudson Bay
Landforms the Ural Mountains, the Painted Desert, the Mesabi Range
Political Units Illinois, the District of Columbia, San Francisco
Public Areas Fort Sumter, Jefferson Memorial, Yosemite National Park
Roads and Highways Michigan Avenue, State Street, Highway 401

Also capitalize **names of sections of the country,** but not compass directions. Capitalize **proper adjectives** derived from names of sections of the country. Do not capitalize adjectives derived from words indicating directions.

Have you ever visited the **W**est?
Our house is west of town.
We traveled north toward Ottawa.
Bruce attended an **E**astern school.

Using Capital Letters Correctly Write capital letters where they are needed above the words in the following sentences.

1. On our trip to the west, we saw the geyser they call old faithful.
2. Charles Lindbergh flew across the atlantic to europe, landing in paris.
3. Early in June we plan to climb castle peak in colorado.
4. First we'll hike up from ashcroft and ski in montezuma basin.
5. Violent typhoons occur in the south china sea, which is really the western arm of the pacific ocean.
6. The blue ridge parkway leads to great smoky mountains national park.
7. You can hike along the appalachian trail from maine to georgia.
8. Did you like the washington monument more than the lincoln memorial?
9. Soldiers from the north and from the south fought the Civil War.
10. It ended with a surrender at appomattox courthouse in virginia in 1865.
11. The arctic circle is about 23 degrees south of the north pole.
12. I know that jackson hole in northwest wyoming is a fertile valley.
13. From the snake river you'll get good views of the teton range.
14. We went fishing in lazy creek, six miles north of interstate 80.
15. There is an important radio astronomy observatory near arecibo, puerto rico.
16. The town of coon rapids is on the mississippi river in minnesota.
17. I would love to visit crete, a greek island in the mediterranean sea.
18. People speak italian in the swiss canton of ticino.

Capitalize all the important words in the **names of organizations and institutions.**

XYZ Corporation	**H**aven **J**unior **H**igh **S**chool	**L**ibrary of **C**ongress
St. **J**ames **H**ospital	**F**ord **F**oundation	**S**mith **C**ompany

Do not capitalize such words as *school, church, college,* and *hospital* when they are not used as names.

Capitalize the **names of historical events, documents, and periods of time.**

World **W**ar I	**D**eclaration of **I**ndependence
Civil **W**ar	**R**enaissance

Capitalize the **names of months, days, and holidays,** but not the names of seasons.

November	**M**emorial **D**ay	**W**ednesday	spring
Saturday	**N**ew **Y**ear's **E**ve	**F**ourth of **J**uly	summer

Using Capital Letters Correctly Write capital letters where they are needed above the words in the following sentences.

1. Much of the great wall of china was rebuilt during the ming dynasty.
2. My sister is looking forward to valentine's day on february 14.
3. Some of us will visit the museum of science and industry on friday.
4. How will the sierra club observe earth day?
5. The holy roman empire was much weaker after the thirty years war.
6. Is there a middle school near kennedy hospital?
7. Yes, skiles middle school is next to the hospital.
8. This summer carla joined the league of women voters.
9. The university of michigan in ann arbor has a good law school.
10. Back in the middle ages, king john of england signed the magna carta.
11. The new york jets and the dallas cowboys will play next week.
12. Last friday, ms. cummings started working for comfort shoes, inc.
13. The adler planetarium will change its program in january.
14. In 1919 the treaty of versailles helped to end world war I.
15. Will acme press publish joe's book about the great depression?
16. I saw a copy of the bill of rights in our public library.
17. In new orleans people celebrate mardi gras with parades.
18. At jones brothers we'll begin observing fire prevention week on monday.

Languages, Peoples, Transportation, and Abbreviations

Capitalize the **names of languages, races, nationalities, and religions,** as well as **adjectives derived from those names.**

Catholicism **S**wiss cheese **E**nglish class **A**frican folk tales

Capitalize the **names of ships, trains, and aircraft.** Capitalize **brand names** of automobiles.

Orient **E**xpress **C**hevrolet ***Q**ueen **E**lizabeth II* the ***H**indenburg*

Capitalize the **abbreviations B.C. and A.D.** and **A.M. and P.M.**

The time was 7:45 **A.M.** The year was **A.D.** 1941.

Using Capital Letters Correctly Write capital letters where they are needed above the words in the following sentences.

1. Hadrian became a roman emperor in a.d. 117.

2. Even though we're irish, our family loves greek food.

3. Last july, lupe traded in her honda and bought a ford.

4. My grandmother sailed on the *queen mary* to visit her scottish friends.

5. A troupe of chinese acrobats is performing at fox memorial stadium.

6. That cajun band from louisiana arrived on a greyhound bus at 2:30 p.m.

7. My father speaks russian and hebrew at work but english at home.

8. We know that islam, judaism, and christianity have much in common.

9. Will the orient express leave paris at 7:15 a.m.?

10. By 800 b.c., the etruscans were living in what is now central italy.

11. The navajos are the largest native american tribe in the united states.

12. The villagers were singing a lutheran hymn in an african language.

13. In haiti the people speak a dialect of french called creole.

14. Was it *apollo 11* that first landed on the moon in july of 1969?

15. Yuki ate an italian dinner before leaving on the concorde at 9 p.m.

16. We had an evening of russian folk dancing and argentine singing.

17. There are large groups of hindus and muslims in india.

18. In a.d. 1492 the *santa maria* arrived in the bahamas.

19. The packard, the duesenberg, and the pierce-arrow were classic automobiles.

20. A new millennium will begin in a.d. 2001.

First Words (I)

Capitalize the **first word of every sentence.**

His mother began her own company.
Will you leave tonight?

Capitalize the **first word of each line in most** poetry.

Among twenty snowy mountains,
The only moving thing
Was the eye of the blackbird.
From "Thirteen Ways of Looking at a Blackbird" by Wallace Stevens

Capitalize the **first word of a direct quotation.**

Mother asked, "**H**ave you seen my umbrella?"

A quotation that is interrupted is called a **divided quotation.** Do not capitalize the first word of the second part of a divided quotation unless it begins a new sentence.

"**A**fter school," she said, "we can go to the library."
"**T**hat's it," said Tony. "**T**hat's the answer."

Using Capital Letters Correctly Write capital letters where they are needed above the words in the following sentences.

1. "after lunch," said sasha, "let's walk uptown."

2. what's in a name? that which we call a rose
by any other word would smell as sweet.
From *Romeo and Juliet* by William Shakespeare

3. "there's no school," explained heather. "it's memorial day."

4. "the egg of today," a proverb says, "is better than the hen of tomorrow."

5. joanie shouted, "here comes the parade!"

6. "three may keep a secret," said benjamin franklin, "if two of them are dead."

7. a harvest mouse goes scampering by
with silver claws and a silver eye.

8. the captain asked, "have you seen anything?"

9. "do you know," tim asked, "the capital of florida?"

10. "of course I do," I replied. "it's tallahassee."

First Words (II)

Capitalize only the **first word in each line of an outline.**

I. **S**olar energy
  A. **C**ollection of heat
    1. **B**y air
    2. **B**y water
  B. **U**se of energy

Capitalize **all important** words in the greeting of a letter.

Dear **S**ir or **M**adam: **D**ear **D**r. **B**arnes:

In the closing of a letter, capitalize only the **first word.**

Sincerely yours, **Y**ours very truly,

Capitalize the **first word, the last word, and all other important words in titles.**

__S__ports __I__llustrated (magazine)
"**T**he **R**aven" (poem)
__W__all __S__treet __J__ournal (newspaper)
"**T**his **L**and **I**s **Y**our **L**and" (song)
__R__aisin in the __S__un (play)
__I__sland of the __B__lue __D__olphins (book)
__F__unniest __H__ome __V__ideos (TV series)
__G__one with the __W__ind (movie)

Using Capital Letters Correctly Write capital letters where they are needed above the words in the following sentences.

1. The newspaper carrier just brought my *chicago sun-times.*

2. dear mr. scott:
I would like to order a subscription to *consumer reports.*

3. very truly yours,

4. Do you ever watch reruns of *star trek* on television?

5. One of my favorite poems is "to a mouse" by Robert Burns.

6. Mort will sing "it's not easy being green" at the concert.

7. I have just finished reading *life on the mississippi.*

8. My subscription to *seventeen* has expired.

9. Be sure to read "the mayoral election" in your copy of *newsweek.*

10. We're going to see *the sound of music* at the high school.

11. III. popular music
  A. american
    1. country and western

12. My mother's favorite film is *singin' in the rain.*

Linking Mechanics and Writing: Capitalization

Imagine that you are planning a party to celebrate a holiday or special event. In the space below, create an invitation. Include at least six of the following kinds of information:

- the name of a holiday
- the name of a person
- the name of an organization or institution
- a nationality
- a title
- a geographical name
- an abbreviation
- a day of the week

Additional Practice: Capitalization

Using Capital Letters Correctly Write capital letters where they are needed above the words in the following sentences.

1. the great revival in european art and learning is called the renaissance.
2. "read this article," dave said. "it's about personal computers."
3. the earliest vietnamese state was formed around a.d. 950 along the red river just south of china.
4. "dad molds the clay," isabel explained, "but mom paints it."
5. in *kid news* I read about a play by neil simon, called *lost in yonkers.*
6. ancestors of the inuit people had come to the western hemisphere by 8000 b.c.
7. "that lake in northern scotland," said uncle ed, "is called loch ness."
8. a soviet space probe, *luna 9,* landed on the moon in february of 1966.
9. many christian and jewish scholars are studying the dead sea scrolls.
10. bret harte wrote "the luck of roaring camp" and other tales about the west.
11. about 950 b.c., david chose solomon to be the next king of israel.
12. from our boeing jet we could see traces of the santa fe trail below.
13. if groundhog day, february 2, is cloudy, can we expect an early spring?
14. it was many and many a year ago,
    in a kingdom by the sea,
    that a maiden there lived whom you may know
    by the name of annabel lee.
    From "annabel lee" by edgar allan poe
15. a muslim is a person who follows the religion of islam.
16. by 550 b.c., civilizations in the mediterranean basin were thriving.

Review: Capitalization

Using Capital Letters Correctly Write capital letters where they are needed above the words in the following sentences.

1. does aunt natalie think the atlanta hawks can beat the chicago bulls?

2. my dad says that the main religions in japan are shinto and buddhism.

3. "i'm lost," i said. "is dead horse canyon near the frying pan river?"

4. w. c. handy, who wrote "st. louis blues," lived in memphis, tennessee.

5. according to archbishop ussher of ireland, the world was created at 9:00 a.m. on october 26 in the year 4004 b.c.

6. the sargasso sea lies between the azores and the west indies.

7. the talmud is a vast collection of writings on jewish law.

8. the kentucky derby will take place at churchill downs on saturday.

9. the vice-president of the united states will go to africa in the fall.

10. one odd corner of the atlantic ocean is called the bermuda triangle.

11. "i wonder," ann said, "what to expect from you on april fool's day."

12. some think the greatest work of the spanish painter picasso is *guernica.*

13. my cousin jerry asked me, "do you know how to juggle?"

14. last wednesday the fbi found counterfeit u.s. and canadian currency.

15. II. how to train your dog

A. kinds of tricks

1. roll over

2. play dead

B. kinds of rewards

16. the koran, the sacred book of the muslims, is written in arabic.

17. the first issue of *action comics,* published in june 1938, is quite rare.

18. j.r.r. tolkien wrote *the fellowship of the ring.*

19. "water, water, everywhere / nor any drop to drink."

20. "i've got the chevy outside," said uncle carl, "and we're ready to go."

End Marks (I)

Use a period at the end of a declarative sentence.

Anton sped down the hill.

Use a period at the end of an imperative sentence expressing mild emotion. If you want to express stronger excitement or emotion, use an exclamation point.

Turn off the radio before you leave.
Watch out!

Use a period at the end of an indirect question.

José asked when the test would be.

Use a period after most abbreviations and after initials.

Mon. (*Monday*) C.P. Snow A.D. (*Anno Domini*) Mr. Davis

Periods are omitted in many abbreviations, such as *rpm, mph,* and *UN.* If you are not sure, use your dictionary.

Put a period after the letters or numbers in an outline or list.

I. Vegetables	1. Clean room.
A. Kinds	2. Mow lawn.
B. Growing season	3. Call Pat.

Using End Marks In the sentences below, supply the missing end marks wherever they are needed.

1. At the end of *Swan Lake*, the audience applauded wildly
2. Maria said the rehearsal for *The Mikado* would begin at 5:30 PM tomorrow
3. Please join us for the field trip to the D T Smith food-processing plant
4. René asked whether he could borrow our blender
5. The invitation read, "Monday, Feb 9, 10:00 AM"
6. II Books
   A Fiction
   B Nonfiction
7. L D Jones drove at 55 mph for 580 yd
8. Stop that terrible noise
9. Leroy quietly answered Ms Hamilton's question
10. In 51–49 and 48–30 BC, Cleopatra was queen of Egypt
11. The homeroom teacher asked why Robert T Able was not in class
12. The ladder is falling—look out

End Marks (II)

Use a question mark at the end of an interrogative sentence.

When is the test**?**   Who rang the bell**?**

Use an exclamation point at the end of an exclamatory sentence.

What a wonderful time we had**!**

Use an exclamation point after an interjection or any other exclamatory expression.

Oh, my**!**
Ouch**!** That hurt**!**

Use an exclamation point after a declarative sentence that you want to emphasize.

That's terrible**!**
You nearly knocked me over**!**

Using End Marks Punctuate the following phrases and sentences by adding the correct end marks.

1. Wow That was a great movie
2. Susan asked if you knew her aunt
3. What an awful smell that is
4. Hurry We may be late
5. Is the bank closed today
6. Help Quick
7. Let's go to the planetarium
8. Tell me about the novel you read
9. Watch out for the flying glass
10. Ouch I guess I'll avoid the hot sand
11. Where were you last Saturday
12. Gosh Who left this mess
13. Stop that child from running into the street
14. Ms. Lawrence asked me if I would help
15. Please return these library books
16. Do you know who my favorite singer is
17. Jeff asked when our next test will be
18. What an amazing story
19. Stop Somewhere ahead there's a thousand-foot drop-off
20. When are we expected for dinner

Commas That Separate Ideas (I)

A compound sentence is a sentence in which independent sentences are joined with a conjunction. Use a comma before the conjunction that joins two sentences in a compound sentence.

The fire alarm rang**,** but it was only a drill.

In a very short compound sentence, it is not necessary to put a comma before *and,* but it is necessary to put a comma before *but* or *or.*

Dorothy raced and she won.
Dorothy raced**,** but she didn't win.

In a sentence with a compound predicate made up of two parts, do not use a comma between the parts. In a compound predicate made up of three parts, use a comma after each of the first two parts.

Sidney read the story and answered the questions.
Sidney read the story**,** answered the questions**,** and wrote a report.

Using Commas Correctly Add commas wherever necessary in the following sentences. Watch for compound predicates. If a sentence is correct, write *C* before it.

______ **1.** The mail carrier brought the magazine but she didn't bring my letter.

______ **2.** I raised my head and then I heard the strange, faint noise.

______ **3.** The coyote looks like a wolf and lives in the prairies.

______ **4.** Did you see the accident or were you looking the other way?

______ **5.** Snow fell but it melted right away.

______ **6.** Darryl has gone but he will return tomorrow.

______ **7.** The manager liked Roger's work and offered him a permanent job.

______ **8.** Everyone in the room carefully watched the card trick but the magician fooled each of them anyway.

______ **9.** Phil studied and he passed.

______ **10.** There are eight colored pencils but four are broken.

______ **11.** May Natalie come here or should we study at her house?

______ **12.** The twins worked together but played apart.

______ **13.** Do you know the metric system or must you learn it?

______ **14.** The plumber ordered a pizza ate it and left the restaurant.

______ **15.** American pioneers moved westward and met many hardships.

______ **16.** This cassette recorder is on sale and it's the only one left.

______ **17.** Put your keys by the door or you might forget them.

______ **18.** Stephanie drank the grapefruit juice finished her salad and began to clean up.

Commas That Separate Ideas (II)

Use a comma after each item in a series except the last. A **series** consists of three or more items of the same kind, written one after the other in a sentence. These items may be verbs, nouns, modifiers, phrases, or other parts of a sentence.

The sheep dog barked, jumped, and rolled over. (verbs)
Sam, Susan, Steve, and Scott went home. (nouns)

Use a comma between adjectives that come before a noun if they do not express a closely related thought.

The forlorn, hungry dog followed us home.

When two adjectives are used together before a noun to express a single idea, do not use a comma between them.

We bought a *shiny red* wagon for my little brother.

Using Commas Add commas where they are needed in the following sentences. If a sentence is correct, write *C* before it.

_____ **1.** The sun rose roosters crowed and the day began.

_____ **2.** The weary Girl Scouts set up camp and made dinner.

_____ **3.** We study history math science and language arts.

_____ **4.** Larry sent out invitations planned the menu decorated the house and waited for the guests.

_____ **5.** The children looked at the little red car going by.

_____ **6.** The nearsighted unsuspecting man was unaware of his narrow escape.

_____ **7.** The wild violent gale whipped the sea into foaming peaks.

_____ **8.** The contestants ran swam and biked all day long.

_____ **9.** The beautiful brown horse leaped over the fence and galloped into the woods.

_____ **10.** The chipmunk scurried across the street into the yard and up the tree.

_____ **11.** Dave Marc and Juan left the building and walked into the schoolyard.

_____ **12.** The short witty comedian made the unfriendly audience laugh.

_____ **13.** Internationally known actors and actresses often work in Paris London and Rome.

_____ **14.** Ms. Field wore a navy blue suit and carried a bulging leather briefcase.

_____ **15.** The cool gentle breeze drifted across the deep still waters of the sea.

_____ **16.** The crisp sunny day beckoned and Keith marched off to meet his friends.

_____ **17.** The students observed sharks eels crabs and lobsters at the aquarium.

_____ **18.** Zulma finished her report typed it up and sat back with a sigh of relief.

Commas That Set Off Special Elements (I)

Use a comma after an introductory word or phrase to separate it from the rest of the sentence.

> No, I don't like spinach.
> Closing his eyes, Bill sat through the horror film.

The comma may be omitted if there would be little pause in speaking.

> At last the game ended.

Use commas before and after interrupters. **Interrupters** are words that break the flow of thought in a sentence.

> This fabric, on the other hand, is preshrunk.
> There are, I believe, three choices.

Using Commas to Set Off Words Correctly Add commas where necessary in the following sentences. Some sentences may be correct.

1. Abraham Lincoln it is said walked twenty miles a day to study law.
2. Running to third I tripped and sprained my ankle.
3. Obviously we couldn't go to the band concert in the rain.
4. Smiling broadly Charlie showed us his loose tooth.
5. Chess as we all know is a game of skill.
6. Finding himself in real danger Joe called for help.
7. Unfortunately the soccer match was canceled.
8. The committee as I said earlier will meet on Tuesday.
9. Pointing her finger the witness identified the defendant.
10. Everyone we were told should go to the safety drill.
11. At last the plane landed.
12. Do you think now that you've seen the problems that you'll finish?
13. Oh I guess so.
14. By the way here's the sweater I borrowed.
15. After all she is your sister.
16. Usually we go to Michigan for our vacation.
17. There is however one condition.
18. Absence as the saying goes makes the heart grow fonder.
19. On the other hand some say that out of sight is out of mind.
20. Well we're getting ahead of our story.

Commas That Set Off Special Elements (II)

Use commas to set off all nouns used in direct address. A **noun used in direct address** is the name or title of a person being spoken to.

Call me**,** Steve**,** if you hear any news.

If the commas are omitted, the sentence is confusing.

Use commas to set off most appositives. An **appositive** is a noun or phrase that identifies the person or thing preceding it.

Judith**,** my aunt**,** is in Florida.
Ann**,** the captain of the team**,** is in my class.

When the appositive is a short name, it is not usually set off by commas.

This is my friend Mary.

Using Commas with Nouns of Direct Address and with Appositives Add commas where necessary in the following sentences.

1. Ms. Cavendish the owner of the business asked our advice.
2. Dad this is my math teacher.
3. Scamper the dog in the yard acts friendly most of the time.
4. Aunt Jan I'd like you to meet my friend Millie.
5. Did you see my skateboard Ron?

Using Commas Rewrite the following sentences, combining each pair into a single sentence by using an appositive.

1. Dr. Tignino is our dentist. She is patient with us.

___

2. The coach is Mr. Fisher. He is a strict man.

___

3. The book on the shelf is *Treasure Island.* It has a leather cover.

___

4. We visited the Art Institute. It is a beautiful building.

___

5. Lorraine has joined the gymnastics squad. She is the new student.

___

Other Uses of the Comma (I)

Use commas to set off explanatory words used with a direct quotation. A **direct quotation** is a restatement of someone's exact words. These exact words are enclosed in quotation marks. **Explanatory words** are words like *Joyce said, Peter asked,* or *Fred shouted.* These words can be placed before, after, or in the middle of the direct quotation.

1. Joyce said**,** "There is the mayor."
2. "I see him**,**" shouted Fred.
3. "The mayor**,**" stated Larissa**,** "has brown hair."

When explanatory words come before a direct quotation, as in the first example, the comma comes after the last explanatory word. In the second example, the explanatory words come after the direct quotation, and the comma is placed after the last word of the quotation. The third example shows the explanatory words separating the quotation. This is called a **divided quotation,** and commas are placed after the last word of the first part and after the explanatory words.

An **indirect quotation,** in which something a speaker says is restated in different words, does not require commas.

Joyce said that she had seen the mayor.

Using Commas with Direct Quotations Add commas wherever necessary in the following sentences. Some sentences are correct.

1. "Well" Deborah sighed "the parade is over."

2. After the accident, the police officer asked us to move our car.

3. "I haven't memorized that poem yet" Joe told Mr. Andrews.

4. Tina asked "Do you know Steven Haines?"

5. "Clean the mud off your shoes" suggested Mom "on the back porch."

6. "Be sure to stay on the path" cautioned the ranger.

7. Dad asked us to clean the garage next weekend.

8. Mayor Jackson asked "How many votes do I need?"

9. "You'd better put that package down" said Len "or you'll hurt yourself."

10. "That's really a great sound" the composer told the string players.

11. Bonnie stated "I promise to tell the whole truth."

12. Bernie said that Alicia can recite the Gettysburg Address.

13. "The weather" announced the forecaster "is unusually cold for this time of year."

14. Several people shouted "Shame, shame!"

15. "Wait for us" directed Ellen "in the lobby."

Other Uses of the Comma (II)

Use commas to separate the parts of dates, addresses, and letters.

In a date, use a comma between the day of the month and the year. If the date is part of a sentence, use another comma after the year. Do not use a comma if only the month and the year are given.

> November 11**,** 1918**,** was Armistice Day.
> Armistice Day was first celebrated in November 1918.

Use a comma to separate the parts of an address. Note that no comma is used before the ZIP code.

> She was born in Buffalo**,** New York**,** and now lives in London**,** England.
> He lives at 1334 Maple Road**,** Williamsville**,** NY 14221.

In friendly letters, use a comma after the greeting. In both friendly and business letters, use a comma after the closing.

> Dear Mom**,**   Very truly yours**,**

Use a comma to separate any sentence parts that might be improperly joined or misunderstood without the comma.

> At night**,** time seems to pass slowly.
> After running**,** the stallions were tired.

Using Commas Correctly Add commas where necessary in the following sentences and phrases.

1. Write to 50 W. Forty-fourth Street New York NY 10036.
2. We're leaving for Minnesota on Thursday July 5.
3. Dear Aunt Helen
4. We'll be living in Albuquerque New Mexico by May 1995.
5. My mom and dad's anniversary is Monday August 6.
6. Sherlock Holmes lived at 221B Baker Street London England.

Using Commas to Avoid Confusion Add commas to the following sentences to make the meaning clear.

1. Inside the wall was crumbled and broken.
2. As he watched four soldiers came in after him.
3. Before coloring her little sister put the other toys away.
4. When he looked underneath the table seemed broken.
5. Instead of just watching my sister played in the softball game.
6. By the time she woke up the neighborhood was quiet.

The Semicolon and the Colon

Use a semicolon to separate the parts of a compound sentence when you do not use a coordinating conjunction.

Valerie saw the car**;** it was stalled.

Use a semicolon to separate items in a series that are already punctuated with commas.

I have pen pals in Nairobi, Kenya**;** Rome**,** Italy**;** and Nome, Alaska.

Use a semicolon between the parts of a compound sentence if these clauses are long or complicated or already contain commas.

Sonny hit a single, a double, and a triple**;** but he also made a throwing error and dropped four fly balls in the outfield.

Use a colon to introduce a list of items, to follow the greeting in a business letter, and to separate hours from minutes in a time expression.

Be here by 11**:**30, and bring the following**:** your book, a pen or pencil, and a supply of paper.
Dear Sir or Madam**:**

Using Semicolons and Colons Correctly Add the correct punctuation marks in the following sentences and phrases.

1. Five runners began the race only one finished.
2. We'll meet at the Indian restaurant at 530 P.M. try to be on time.
3. Dear Professor
4. During the night, cars raced, screeched, and honked two tomcats meowed and yowled and a police siren blared.
5. You'll need these items poster board, magic markers, and spray paint.
6. For the bowling party, James invited Lila, Nick, Julio, and Gloria and I asked Martina and Jules.
7. At 301 P.M. on Tuesday, the power failed everybody went home.
8. Several of the students made clocks mine was the only one that ran.
9. The police obtained the following information about each suspect name, address, phone number, and occupation.
10. We'll have a full moon on Tuesday April 6 Wednesday May 5 and Friday June 4.
11. Call me at 230 P.M. tomorrow ask me again then.
12. Patti goes to the dentist tonight Peter will go on Saturday.
13. Marguerite grows tomatoes, cucumbers, and squash steams them slightly and serves them with rice, peppers, and spices.
14. Amanda tried to call home the telephone was out of order.
15. The mail should get here around 130 P.M. maybe my check will arrive.

The Hyphen

Use a hyphen to divide a word at the end of a line.

Kristen and Lisa are swimming in tomorrow's meet.

Use a hyphen in a compound adjective that precedes the word it modifies.

Mark wore a well-tailored suit to the dance.

Use hyphens in compound numbers from twenty-one through ninety-nine and in fractions.

Forty-three students tried out for parts in the school play.
We need a two-thirds majority to pass the resolution.

Spell certain compound nouns with hyphens. Use a dictionary if you are not sure how to punctuate a compound.

vice-president great-aunt

Using Hyphens Correctly Add hyphens where necessary in the following sentences.

1. Michael Jordan's number is twenty three.
2. Have you ever seen a brown eyed cat?
3. A three fourths majority of all states is necessary for approval of an amendment to the Constitution.
4. I gave the clerk a dollar, and I got twenty five cents in change.
5. Her gymnastics routine consisted of several flip flops, handsprings, and somersaults.
6. Esther and Tracy went to the game, and in the sixth in
ning, they were lucky enough to catch a baseball.
7. That museum is on Forty seventh Street.
8. The recipe called for one third cup of milk.
9. Susan is vice president of the Latin Club.
10. All the kids liked the merry go round.
11. Some cars with eight cylinder engines are being recalled.
12. She came from a well to do family.
13. I am left handed, but my brother is right handed.
14. My great grandmother is eighty one years old.
15. Does your sister in law have a ten speed bike?

The Apostrophe (I)

Use an apostrophe to show possession. The **possessive form** of a noun indicates that the person or thing named owns or possesses something.

To form the possessive of a singular noun, add *'s.*

friend + **'s** = friend's   Chris + **'s** = Chris's

To form the possessive of a plural noun that ends in *s,* add only an apostrophe.

nurses + **'** = nurses'   cousins + **'** = cousins'

To form the possessive of a plural noun that does not end in *s,* add *'s.*

men + **'s** = men's   deer + **'s** = deer's

Forming the Possessives of Nouns Correctly Write the possessive forms of the following nouns.

1. child ____________	**17.** calf ____________
2. Charles ____________	**18.** woman ____________
3. robin ____________	**19.** pony ____________
4. country ____________	**20.** turkey ____________
5. girls ____________	**21.** boys ____________
6. fish ____________	**22.** suburbs ____________
7. monkeys ____________	**23.** dog ____________
8. dentist ____________	**24.** school ____________
9. cities ____________	**25.** women ____________
10. Ms. Klaus ____________	**26.** baby ____________
11. game ____________	**27.** elf ____________
12. students ____________	**28.** presidents ____________
13. priest ____________	**29.** secretary ____________
14. electrician ____________	**30.** carpenters ____________
15. mice ____________	**31.** states ____________
16. lawyers ____________	**32.** hostess ____________

The Apostrophe (II)

Use an apostrophe to show where letters are omitted in a contraction. A **contraction** is a shortened form of a word or group of words. An apostrophe is used in a contraction to show where one or more letters have been omitted.

we are = we're	where is = where's
she is = she's	they are = they're
here is = here's	cannot = can't
there is = there's	could not = couldn't
I would = I'd	will not = won't
we will = we'll	was not = wasn't
they will = they'll	would not = wouldn't
it is = it's	who is = who's

Do not confuse these contractions with pronouns that sound the same:

They're going to the store. *It's* your turn.
Their store is on the corner. *Its* time has come.

Use apostrophes to form the plurals of letters, figures, and words used as words. To form these plurals, add *'s*.

Sheila wrote *7*'s and *9*'s in a unique way.
Ray's writing was full of *and*'s.

Using Apostrophes Correctly Add apostrophes wherever they are needed.

1. Well see the Angels play when theyre in town.
2. I cant do it, and I wont.
3. Whos the student who used three *but*s in one sentence?
4. Theres nobody here; its lonely.
5. Wheres the girl whose coat is on this chair?
6. Ill help you remember that *commit* has two *m*s.

Choosing the Correct Word Underline the correct words in parentheses.

1. (There's, Theirs) a swallow taking (it's, its) bath in that puddle.
2. Do you know (who's, whose) umbrella that is?
3. (It's, Its) been fun staying at (they're, their) house.
4. (You're, Your) going skating, and (they're, their) going to the show.
5. (We'll, Well) stay for dinner if (you're, your) cooking.
6. (They're, Their) going to attend (you're, your) party.

Quotation Marks (I)

Use quotation marks to enclose direct quotations. A **direct quotation** is a restatement of someone's exact words, and the quotation marks show where those words begin and end. Quotation marks are not used with indirect quotations.

> Lionel asked, "How often does leap year occur?"
> Lionel asked how often leap year occurs.

When a direct quotation is interrupted by explanatory words, enclose each part of the quotation in quotation marks. Begin the second part of a divided quotation with a small letter unless it is the beginning of a sentence.

> "When you are ready," said Amy, "we'll eat lunch."
> "I'm ready," said Juanita. "Let's eat now."

Using Quotation Marks Correctly In the sentences below, add quotation marks where they are needed.

1. Paul answered, The capital of California is Sacramento.
2. I like most fruit, said Kelly, but I don't like Bosc pears.
3. The rain has stopped, announced Elena. Now we can play softball.
4. Larry asked, Does anyone have a pencil that I can borrow?
5. Here is your change, said the cashier.
6. Yoshi asked when the chemistry exam was.

Writing Quotations Correctly Rewrite the following sentences correctly, adding quotation marks and capitalizing words where necessary.

1. Here is the book report, said Hugh, that I wrote yesterday.

   ____

2. I enjoy your piano playing, said Tanya. please play another piece.

   ____

3. We were on time, Lynne protested, but the school bus was late.

   ____

4. It was a close game, said the catcher. fortunately, we won.

   ____

5. When the dance recital was over, Lisa wrote, the audience applauded wildly.

   ____

Place quotation marks outside commas and end marks following direct quotations.

> "It has begun to snow," said Andy.
> "The movie was enjoyable," said Chen, "but I have seen better."

Use quotation marks outside exclamation points and question marks if those marks are part of the quotation itself. Place quotation marks inside exclamation points and question marks if they are not part of the quotation.

> Greta shouted, "Watch out!"
> Thank goodness I heard her say "Watch out"!
> Sam asked, "When does the library close?"
> Did you reply, "The library closes at 5:00 P.M."?

Using Quotation Marks Correctly In the sentences below, add quotation marks where they are needed.

1. Did Ms. Ames say, There will be a quiz tomorrow?
2. Stacey asked, In what mountain range is Pikes Peak?
3. When the campgrounds closed, said Nancy, we went home.
4. Where did you buy that hat? asked Ron.
5. Did Harry say Look out! or Excuse me?

Writing Quotations Correctly Rewrite each of the following sentences correctly, adding quotation marks, end marks, and capital letters where necessary.

1. Did you borrow my sweatshirt, asked Tim, or did I lose it

   ____

2. Jayne shouted, Hurray, we won

   ____

3. We went to the store, said Kera unfortunately, it wasn't open

   ____

4. Did Marvin say, I'd like your autograph

   ____

5. How dreadful that he didn't even say I'm sorry

   ____

Quotation Marks (III)

A **dialogue** is a conversation between two or more people. When you are writing a dialogue, begin a new paragraph every time the speaker changes, and use quotation marks for all direct quotations.

> "The forecaster said it would snow today," said Jan. "I hope there is a big storm."
>
> "Yes, I'd like that too," replied Kyle. "I can't wait to try out my new skis on the slopes."

Use quotation marks to set off the titles of short works: book chapters, short stories, reports, articles, songs, and poems.

> "Home on the Range"
> "The Legend of Sleepy Hollow" by Washington Irving
> "Primer Lesson" by Carl Sandburg

Underline the titles of longer works: books, magazines, motion pictures, television series, plays, musical compositions, and paintings. Also underline the names of ships, airplanes (but not the type of plane), spacecraft, and trains.

> The Adventures of Huckleberry Finn
> Fiddler on the Roof
> It's a Wonderful Life
> Newsweek

Using Quotation Marks in Dialogue Punctuate the dialogues below by adding quotation marks where needed. Insert paragraph signs (¶) to show where new paragraphs should begin.

1. Did you go to the jazz concert last Friday? asked Samantha. Yes, I did, replied Karen. I enjoyed it very much. I especially liked the pieces by Charlie Parker that the band played. So did I, said Samantha. I thought the band played very well.
2. We're almost there, said Dad. How much longer will it be? asked Jill. Oh, about thirty minutes, replied Dad. Before you know it, we'll be at the campsite. I can't wait, said Jill. I've been looking forward to this for a long time.

Punctuating Titles Correctly Punctuate the following titles of works, adding quotation marks or underlining the titles as appropriate.

1. Casey at the Bat (poem)
2. The Star-Spangled Banner (song)
3. Sixty Minutes (TV series)
4. Mona Lisa (painting)
5. The Necklace (short story)
6. The Dog That Bit People (essay)
7. Carmen (opera)
8. The Wizard of Oz (movie)
9. Romeo and Juliet (play)
10. The Primal Screen (article)

Linking Mechanics and Writing: Punctuation

Imagine that you are the editor of the school newspaper. A reporter has turned in this story. Correct the 33 errors in punctuation by using proofreading marks. On the lines below the story, write a new paragraph, one that tells about the results of the Slammer-Titan game. Include a quotation, a sentence that contains a series of items, and a sentence that requires a colon.

Slammers Beat Lions

The champion Slammers barely defeated the Lions 34–32 in the Middleburg Jr High gym last Friday, afternoon. The game the first held in the new gym was the fifth straight win for the Slammers!

Mark Fitzpatrick, known as Mr. Slam dunked eight baskets. He scored a total of 19 points. Other Slammer scorers were Tom Washington 8 points; Linda Krevitz 8 points and C C Mendolan 4 points. High scorers for the Lions were Pete Falzone 12 points, Kim Chei 10 points and Buddy Hewett 6 points.

Next Saturday Feb 4 the undefeated Slammers will meet the Titans. The Titan captain Penny Zeska said after Fridays game, "The Slammers are great but theyre not unbeatable. Were the team thats going to end their winning streak!'

In answer to Zeskas boast, Fitzpatrick replied "Well just see about that wont we.

Punctuating Correctly All of the punctuation marks have been omitted from the following paragraphs. Rewrite the paragraphs, using correct punctuation.

Jack exclaimed We wont have dinner until 1200 midnight unless we all hurry and get camp set up Mark and Bill you set up the tent Craig you start the fire and Jerry you finish unloading the car

What are you going to do Jack asked Bill

Commanders usually dont do any work themselves however Ill help by lighting the lantern replied Jack

Thanks Jack said one of the other boys sarcastically but we already have the perfect job for you you are in charge of cleanup

Review: Punctuation

Punctuating Correctly Punctuate the following sentences and phrases correctly, using all the punctuation marks you have studied.

1. Mr Thomas J Ts father took us to the auto show on July 15
2. Wow said Arnie What a treat it would be to spend all day looking around town
3. When we got there about 200 PM the parking lot was three fourths filled and we had to walk miles
4. After applauding the audience suddenly grew quiet
5. Randy Sarah and Pete my cousin stayed for the second show
6. We decided to bring the following things for our picnic sandwiches potato salad watermelon and fruit salad
7. The six of us however couldnt decide on a restaurant
8. Yes the park pavilion will be free on the twenty ninth of June Ive been told
9. We thought of going to the beach we changed our minds though when we found it was going to rain
10. Did you ever go to that childrens camp when you were young
11. You can write to the publishing company at 230 Park Ave New York City NY 10017
12. I was born on December 16 1980 in Seattle said Sheila
13. Hyun asked Is that a new outfit youre wearing Ron
14. When Tim saw his grade he cried out Good grief
15. If you write to your grandmother said Paula can you dot your *i*s cross your *t*s and write neatly
16. I Neil Wong
    A His music
    B His acting
17. After one quick tiring game Rebecca and Laurie walked downtown bought stationery birthday cards books and records and met Andrea at a restaurant
18. Marcia found her glasses they were in her pocket it seems
19. Sandy asked us to dinner and we had a long interesting conversation
20. What a funny ending

Skills Assessment 4

Handbooks
46–47

Directions One or more of the underlined sections in the following sentences may contain an error in grammar, usage, punctuation, spelling, or capitalization. Write the letter of each incorrect section. Then rewrite the section correctly. If there is no error in an item, write *E.*

Example The original skid row was an area in Seattle,
A B
Washington, where logs skidded down a slope to the
C
first sawmill on Puget sound. No error
D E
Answer D—Puget Sound

1. Washington Irving, the author of the story "Rip Van Winkle," served
A B C
as a U.S. minister to Spain. No error
D E

2. Duke Ellington said of Louis Armstrong, "He was born poor, died
A B
rich and hurt no one in between". No error
C D E

3. Maya Lin designed the Vietnam veterans memorial in Washington, DC,
A B C
and the Civil Rights Memorial in Montgomery, Alabama. No error
D E

4. "I think that science fiction and fantasy," said Ray Bradbury, "Offer the
A B
livelyest, freshest approaches to many of our problems today."
C D
No error
E

5. Sherlock Holmes's ability to solve crimes fascinates readers. This
A
amazing detective appeared in four novels and fifty six short stories
B C D
by Arthur Conan Doyle. No error
E

6. Three of the oldest zoos still in existence are located in Vienna, Austria;
A B C
Paris, France, and Madrid, Spain. No error
D E

7. John Muir founded the sierra club in 1892; members of this
A B C
organization work to protect the environment. No error
D E

8. Most cowboy's horses belonged to ranch owners, but a few of the cowboys owned his horses. No error
(A: cowboy's; B: owners, but; C: his; D: horses.; E: No error)

9. In the 1940s, John H Johnson, the founder of *Ebony* magazine, began his publishing career with $500. No error
(A: John H Johnson,; B: magazine,; C: ,; D: began; E: No error)

10. Whales have no sense of smell. Most species dont see very good, although their sense of hearing is very keen. No error
(A: smell.; B: species; C: dont; D: good,; E: No error)

11. Jesse, have you seen the exhibit of armor from the Middle Ages? It's on display at the Art Institute of Chicago. No error
(A: Jesse,; B: Middle Ages?; C: It's; D: Art Institute of Chicago.; E: No error)

12. The *calypso,* Jacques Cousteau's ship is a floating laboratory. Divers take pictures of ocean life, and the scientists on board analyze the photos. No error
(A: *calypso,*; B: ship is; C: life,; D: photos.; E: No error)

13. My family and I help save natural resources. By recycling household waste items. These items include: glass bottles, aluminum cans, and newspapers. No error
(A: I; B: resources. By; C: These; D: include:; E: No error)

14. "Why is the North Star used to find North?" Maurice asked. "All of the other stars seem to move because of the rotation of the earth." No error
(A: North Star; B: North?"; C: move; D: earth."; E: No error)

15. When muslims pray, they kneel on rugs. These rugs always have an arch woven into their pattern. No error
(A: muslims; B: kneel; C: always; D: have; E: No error)

Proofreading Practice: Understanding Sentences

Writing Sentences Correctly Read the passage below. Then use proofreading marks to correct all errors in capitalization, punctuation, spelling, and usage. Look especially for sentence fragments and run-on sentences.

An elegant coach has long been a symbol of power and position for centuries Kings and Queens have paraded through there kingdoms in royal coaches. In the United States, presidents have also used special vehicles for ceremonial and official occasions. Since 1789 every president except Thomas Jefferson and James Monroe have used a "presidential coach"

George Washington begun the tradition when he adoptted his wife's carriage as the official state coach her Penn carriage had been made in London. It was a gold-trimmed wooden coach with a round bottom. A leather roof, glass windows and a leopard-skin driver's seat trimmed in red and gold lace. Washington beleived a show of elagance ensured that the president of the United States would be treated with dignity.

For years the presidential coaches were made in europe. In fact, none was made in America. Until the term of Millard Fillmore. His dark green, custom-made Clarence coach a gift it had silver lamps on the coachman's box, blue silk curtains for the windows, and the New York State coat of arms painted on the door.

Until 1909 most presidents used there own carriages. Or carraiges that they had recieved as gifts. William h. Taft was the first president to ride in a vehicle provided by the Goverment. Tafts "presidential coach" was a 1911 White steamer. A seven-passenger touring car powered by a steam engine that cost $4,000. Taft was usually accompanyied by three cars carring Secret Service Agents and by two police officers on motorcycles.

Eventually horse-drawn presidential coaches were replaced by limousines. Instead of gold trim and lace curtains, modern presidential cars are equiped with the most up to date technological devices. These cars provide the ultimate in safety, security and comfort. After all, today as in the time of George Washington, a president's "coach" serves as a symbol of the highest office in the country. A very impressive symbol indeed!

Proofreading Practice: Using Nouns

Using Nouns Correctly Read the personal narrative below. Then use proofreading marks to correct all errors in capitalization, punctuation, spelling, and grammar. Pay special attention to the use of nouns.

Recently my classmates and me took part in an outdoor-education program at Camp Wahinipa. The camp is located in the Mountains. Of White Oaks state park. All the buildings are old log cabins built back in the 1940s by the Army corps of engineers.

It was sunny but cold on the day we arrived we were glad we had our scarfs, hats, and gloves. First the camp directer divided the students into six teams. I was assigned to the Green team. Our leaders were Carmen and Vic. They passed out backpacks and sack lunchs and explained that we would be seting out on a Scavenger Hunt. For the rest of the day we hiked through the woods in search of leaves, berrys, feathers, and other things on our list. my partner and me even spotted two deers and a family of foxs. We also found the skeletons of two mice! Carmen and Vic shivered when we showed them the skeletons but everyone else thought they were awesome. That night we played games, ate popcorn, and singed songs around a fire.

The next day we visited Dr Wes' Science class. It was fascinating. We performed experments, using things we had collected the day before. Later we went orienteering. Orienteering is a timed cross-country race. The participants use a compass and a map to follow the course. Some kids couldn't tell North from South. After a hour or so. Our teams' efforts paid off and we were let lose to follow the coarse on our own. Lucky, no one got lost! After dinner some of us pleadded to go on a night hike. As we walked, Carmen told us about a spirit that once haunted the woods. Suddenly a ghostly figure appeared from behind a tree and ran howling into the woods. Everyone screamed later we discovered that our "ghost" was one of the leaders dressed in a sheet. We all had a good laugh and went to bed.

The next day it was time to leave. We said our goodbyes, but no body wanted to go back to the City. I know I will always remember this trip!

Proofreading Practice: Using Pronouns

Choosing the Correct Pronoun Read the play review below. Then use proofreading marks to correct all errors in capitalization, punctuation, spelling, and grammar. Pay close attention to the correct use of pronouns.

There are not many plays that are suited to we teenagers, but this week I attended a play I can highly recommend. An exiting and unusual new play called "Nowhere to Turn" has just opened at the Center Stage Theater. The plot centers on two struggling teenage artists, Trina and Arturo, and there attempts to deal with the world in which they live. Both try to escape his or her world through his or her art.

Trina is a quiet, serious girl who dreams of becoming a muralist. Her father died when she was nine and now her and the rest of her family is struggling to survive. Trina's difficult life makes her wonder if she can meet her goals.

Arturo is a handsome risk-taker who acts as if everything in life is a joke. His friends are impressed by he and his attitude, but we soon learn that his appearance is a cover for his sadness and feelings of worthlessness. Arturo feels worthwhile only when he is working on his art.

The main characters first meet at a community center. In the beginning neither like the other, but over time the two become close friends. Then something happens that threatens their friendship and the fulfilment of their dreams. At this point the scripted play ends and the audience is invited to come up with ways for the main character's to resolve they're conflicts. The best solution, as determined by a vote of the audience, is then brought to life by the cast to end the play.

The lead players, Rita Cruz and Tony Smith, whom are both new to the theater, made we audience members really share Trina's and Arturo's frustrations. Each relys on their personal experiences to create a realistic character. Their improvised ending was pure genious. Many viewers told how they theirselves had dealt with similar conflicts. In fact, I think the play helped me understand more about other people's problems. Don't just take my opinion; see for yourself!

Proofreading Practice: Using Verbs

Using Verbs Correctly Read the personal narrative below. Then use proofreading marks to correct all errors in capitalization, punctuation, spelling, and grammar. Pay special attention to the use of verbs.

For decades now, our town has celebrated the start of the New Year by holding a huge winter festival. Each festival has it's memorable moments, but this year's was one our family will never forget. The weather conditions were perfect; a thick blanket of fresh white snow laid on the ground. My favorite event was the ice-sculpting competition. Mom and me helped to prepare the blocks of ice for the sculptors. In the past, the ice had been took from the frozen parts of the river. This year, however, the weather was so warm that only a small part of the river had froze over by the time of the festival. To solve the problem, the ice committee builded several large molds and made ice blocks. Slowly and carefully we poured water into each eight-foot mold. Then we left the water freeze. It wasn't until a day or two later that my mom asked us if we seen her wedding ring. She didn't remember lying it anywhere, but the ring was nowhere to be found.

On the day of the competition the ring was still missing. Mom could talk of nothing else. As her and I sat up each ice block strait and secure for the sculptors, I joked that maybe her ring had fell into one of the ice molds. Suddenly mom set down, and her eyes got as round as saucers. "Oh, Pat, she cried as she grabbed me by the sholders, I bet you're right! Quick, lets check!" It was to late. The contestants were arriving. Then I got an idea. I run to the judges and shared our suspicions. The solution was easy. A prize would be given not only to the best sculptor but also to the person who found the ring. Mr. Garcia blowed his whistle, and the competition begun. Near the end of the day, the ring was found as one of the artists was carving the tale feathers of a giant swan. The sculptor got his prize, and mom weared her ring home.

Later, in the warmth of our kitchen, we ate apple fritters and drunk hot apple cider to celebrate. Mom had ate three apple fritters before she realized she had been so hungry.

Proofreading Practice: Using Adjectives

Using Adjectives Correctly Read the consumer report that follows. Then use proofreading marks to correct all errors in capitalization, punctuation, spelling, and grammar. Watch for errors in the use of adjectives.

If you plan to "pop for" popcorn for your next party, which brand should you buy. Me and my friends decided to find out. We wanted to test one generic brand and the three top sellers. so we choosed Penny Pincher's generic popcorn, Video Time popcorn Hollywood Star gourmet popcorn, and Colonel Popper's popcorn. Each of the four brands were judged for flavor, quantity (number of popped kernels), and cost. All were prepared both by the traditional method and by the air-pop method. One half cup of kernels was used for each test.

Flavor According to our reviewers, Colonel Poppers Popcorn tastes better no matter which method was used. Hot or cold, every popped kernel had a sweet, Midwestern corn taste. Hollywood Star gourmet popcorn came in second. Although its U.S.-grown and mexican grown multicolored kernels were tastey when hot, they lost flavor when cool. The baddest popcorn was Penny Pincher's. One reviewer complained "This here popcorn tastes like those plastic things used to pack gifts" Video Time popcorn tasted more better then plastic, but it lacked sweetness.

Quantity Surprisingly, Hollywood Star gourmet popcorn recieved top marks in this category. Only 5 of the 378 kernals remained unpopped. Colonel Popper's tied with Video Time for second place, with 12 unpopped kernals. Penny Pincher's came in last, with one quarter of the kernels failing to pop.

Cost Penny Pincher's popcorn cost the least per pound, but ended up being the more costly of the group because of the number of unpopped kernels. The prices of the other three Brands were about the same.

Overall, therefore, Colonel Popper's popcorn is the better buy. Its flavor and texture are excelent, and it provides a lot of pops for the money.

Proofreading Practice: Using Adverbs

A. Using Adverbs Correctly Read the paragraph below. Then use proofreading marks to correct all errors in capitalization, punctuation, spelling, and grammar.

Holly was real nervous. Today would be her first time on skates. Since the acsedent. Had her ankle healed good enough to support her. Holly clenched her teeth tightly, straightened her shoulders, and stepped carefully onto the ice. Well, here goes nothing, she thought. Hesitant, she pushed off with her left foot. She glided slowly and shakily toward her partner Mike. "Keep going, Holly. Your skating good," Mike said encouraging. Holly knew she was not skateing very well yet, but she appreciated the support. Together, the pair began to move more quick across the rink. There still isn't no pain, Holly thought happily. Holly's eyes shinned bright as she realized that with a little work her and Mike might make the olympic qualifying trials after all.

B. Using Adverbs Read the following interview between a student reporter and the star of the local baseball team. Then use proofreading marks to correct all errors.

Question: Well, Bubba, today the buzzards lost the first game of the season. You must feel badly. What happened.

Answer: First of all, Jack. We weren't never focused on winning; we were mainly concerned with not getting beeten. We was on the defensive from the start; therefore, we played poor. We really needed to act more aggressive. We should of moved more quicker. Also, we should have hit more powerfully. Even Starman couldn't hit one into the Outfield. We played terrible.

Question: What do you think caused this unusual lack of concentration?

Answer: Well, I'm embarassed to say it, but we were afraid of the Eagles. Their a Buzzard's worstest nightmare, you know! They're big, bold, brainy, and fast.

Question: I hope you have more better luck tomorrow against the Boomtown Bluebirds. Do you predict a win?

Answer: Ha we can't play any more worse than we did today. Yes, I think you can look forward to an exciting win against the Bluebirds.

Proofreading Practice: Using Prepositions, Conjunctions, and Interjections

A. Using Prepositions, Conjunctions, and Interjections Correctly Read the following passage from a fairy tale. Then use proofreading marks to correct all errors in capitalization, punctuation, spelling, and grammar.

Long ago, across the ocean there lived a boy. With dark, curly hair and eyes the color of the sea. He lived in a small wood hut with his father near the shore. Each morning the boy would sit and stare at the horizon while his father prepared the fishing nets. Then the boy and the man would row out to sea slowly and silently. Neither spoke, but they're thoughts were the same. Where was the mother whom had sailed away and never returned? Oh how they longed to know if she was still alive!

One day a dolphin rised to the surface beside the boy and man with a locket in his mouth. "Wow said the boy that look like mother's locket. dolphin from whom did you get that?" The dolphin just said, follow me, please.

B. Editing Prepositions, Conjunctions, and Interjections Read the plot summary below. Then proofread it for errors in capitalization, punctuation, spelling, and grammar.

The Power Pals receive a mysterious message on their computer. Their Teacher and mentor had been captured by the Evil Evilyn, whoose hideout is in the dessert. The Power Pals decide between themselfs that all five of them must go to save ms. Jones in no time they travel across mesa azul and over the river of Doom until they finally reach the desert. Along the way. They must battle giant scorpions, rock slides, and killer fish that almost eat our heros. Inside the hideout the Power Pals must outsmart the guards and gain access to Evilyn's command center for a time Evilyn's mind-bending powers trick our heros into fighting among themselves but they soon band together and confront Evilyn. A battle of wills begins among Evilyn and Crystal, the strongest of the power pals, but Crystal's friends combine their powers to help her together they save the day.

Proofreading Practice: Using Compound and Complex Sentences

Correcting Compound and Complex Sentences Read the article below. Then use proofreading marks to correct all errors in capitalization, punctuation, spelling, and grammar. Watch for sentence sense.

The term "Wild West" probly brings to mind names such as Jesse James Nat Love, Pat Garrett, and Buffalo Bill. There are also however women whose names should be rememberred as part of this colorful period in US history. Two of them frontierswomen were Annie Oakley and Calamity Jane.

Annie Oakley was born Phoebe Anne Moses in Darke County, Ohio. She learned to shoot a gun at the age of eight. Used her hunting skills to help support her family. Eventually, this young sharpshooter begun to compete in shooting contests. It was at such an exhibition that she met and defeated Frank Butler, a professional marksman who she married in 1876. Annie's fame as a sharpshooter grew; and in 1885 she joined Buffalo Bill's Wild West Show. She remained with the show untill 1901. When she resigned after being injured in a train accident. During World War I, Annie Oakley served her Country well she gave shooting exhibitions and taught servicemen to shoot. Although Annie Oakley is often portrayed as an outspoken tomboy. She was really a quiet, simple person who enjoyed needlepoint and other handicrafts.

Calamity Jane, who's real name was Martha Cannary. Was born near Princeton, Missouri in 1852. She got her nickname from her habit of warning men that to offend her was to court calamity, that is, to court disaster. Calamity Jane was a rugged individualist who became a skilled horsewoman and sharpshooter. Never one to live by Society's rules. She dressed in men's clothing and led a wild life. Some stories say that she even served as a scout for Colonel Custer. During the gold rush of 1878, Calamity Jane was praised as a heroine for treating victims of a smallpox epidemic in Deadwood South Dakota where she lived. She went on to appear in several Wild west shows she died in 1903.

Proofreading Practice: Subject-Verb Agreement

Correcting Subject and Verb Agreement Read the narrative below. Then use proofreading marks to correct all errors in capitalization, punctuation, spelling, and grammar. Make sure that subjects and verbs agree.

Julie and I are horseback riders who help children with special needs learn to ride. An average day at our stable starts very early. Here comes the children. Many wear leg braces or drive wheelchairs. Is any body scarred No every one wants to be first!

An adult trainer and a parent lifts each child in turn onto a horse. A slender nine-year-old boy in jeans and a flannel shirt drops his crutchs as he is lifted onto the back of a caramel-colored Palomino. Once in place, the boy sits proud and expectantly he steadys himself with the saddle horn. "Girls you take Joey and Blaze," calls the instructor. Julie and I hurry over to Joeys side. Julie, who is older and more experienced than I, lead Blaze. I walk along side the horse so that Joey don't fall. Around the ring goes the horse and its rider, with Julie and me close at hand. We joke and laugh but we also teach Joey the proper way to ride. It is hard for Joey to learn some of the cues and techniques, needed to controll the horse because Joey's leg muscles are weak. Joey, like most of the other children, sometimes get frustrated, but he keeps trying. Neither Julie nor I lets him cheat. He must give each cue correct if he wants to control Blaze. There is some teams who are allowed to leave the ring on trail rides. Joey pleads to go out on the trails too but he does'nt ride good enough yet. No one is allowed out of the ring until they pass a test, so Joey and us just keep working.

All to soon the lesson is over. Near the fence sit the next class, eagerly waiting. Joey hugs Blaze, then Julie, then me. Neither Joey nor his friends wants to leave. Most of the children tells us that riding horses makes them feel powerful and free. We know that it also helps them develop coordination, and self-esteem. Julie and I like the hugs and smiles we get. We also like feeling useful.

Proofreading Practice: Capitalization

Capitalizing Words Correctly Read the letter below. Then use proofreading marks to correct all errors in capitalization, punctuation, spelling, and usage. Pay special attention to the use of capital letters.

21 Manor road

Turner's Cross

Cork City, Ireland

July 13, 19—

Dear mom, dad, Jim, and Kate,

Meeting my Pen pal John was like meeting a lost brother! John is a taller and funnyer then I expected. I'm even beginning to understand his Irish accent. We are having a great time together!

I arrived at Cork Airport last Friday at 8:30 a.m. the trip from New york took ten hours. John and the whole Sheehan Family was there to greet me. The sun was shineing when I landed, and John's Mom joked that I must have brung the good weather. Unfortunately it has rainned every day since then.

As you can see from my photos, the Sheehan's live in a beautiful new row house South of the Lee river. I am sharing a bedroom with John. He must usually be as disorganized as I am, because at least once a day his Dad says jokingly, "how tidy your room looks today, son."

Every day we play Soccer and explore the City. We visited Dr. Sheehan's lab at University college and rang the bells at Shandon. Did you know that Cork city is over 800 years old? Many of the older buildings near the art gallery are being rennovated. John's Grandfather is helping to renovate the School he went to as a boy.

This morning we are going to watch a Hurling match and this afternoon we are going to tour Blarney castle. I'll telephone on Saturday, July 23, at Noon.

Your Loving Son,

Kevin

Proofreading Practice: Punctuation

Correcting Punctuation Read the school newspaper article that follows. Use proofreading marks to correct all errors in capitalization. Look especially for punctuation errors.

An Egg-citing Assignment

Last Wenesday in Cutter's Woods, three seventh graders were collecting insects for Science class when they came across several large eggs buried in the dirt. "The eggs were gorgeous!" explained Amy Grant, who was the first to see them, "They was bigger than goose eggs Each one was gold and silver with black markings."

Amy was trying to catch a beetle when she discovered the first egg she called Ana Cruz and Rachel Lyons, who were bug hunting nearby. "At first we were more curious than excited. Our fingers were shaking as we losened the egg from the dirt. Found four more eggs in a velvet nest. Ana shook one of the eggs and said it sounded full of money. Then we all started shouting and dancing," said Amy.

Ana Cruz continued the story that was when we forgot about the bugs and begun wondering what the eggs were made of and how they came to be burried in the woods? Who would bother making and decorating the eggs only to hide them in the dirt? We came up with some amuseing possibilities, but we really had no answers. Then Rachel our resident detective started examining the markings on the eggs."

"Yeah, a lot of the markings were wore off, but one egg had the first two lines of the poem All That Is Gold by J. R. R. Tolkien in very small letters around the middle. I knew the poem because we had red it in class" added Rachel Lyons. The girls said it was at this that point that they talked about whether to bring the eggs to the police; to the Hospital to be X-rayed or to Dr Cummings an Archaeologist at Dewey college.

For now the girl's eggs are in a safe at the Blair Police Station. The content of the eggs are still a mystery if no one claims the eggs by September, 7, the girls would get to keep them. Anyone with information about the eggs should contact Det. Julia Smith Blair Police Department, 2468 Cedar Road, Blair ID, 12345.